T0128420

GOD CHOSE US.
WHAT'S NEXT?

Revised Edition

ELAINE L. BUTLER

WESTBOW
PRESS®
A DIVISION OF THOMAS NELSON
& ZONDERVAN

WestBow Press books may be ordered through booksellers or by contacting:

WestBow Press
A Division of Thomas Nelson & Zondervan
1663 Liberty Drive
Bloomington, IN 47403
www.westbowpress.com
844-714-3454

Scripture quotations marked CSB have been taken from the Christian Standard Bible®, Copyright © 2017 by Holman Bible Publishers. Used by permission. Christian Standard Bible® and CSB® are federally registered trademarks of Holman Bible Publishers.

ISBN: 978-1-6642-8173-8 (sc)
ISBN: 978-1-6642-8175-2 (hc)
ISBN: 978-1-6642-8174-5 (e)

Library of Congress Control Number: 2022919716

Print information available on the last page.

WestBow Press rev. date: 11/18/2022

To my Lord and Savior, Jesus Christ, the one and only creator and sustainer. He is always putting me on the potter's wheel. When He does, I come out stronger.

To my special cheerleaders: Cathy Fialon, my husband, and my family, who put up with my long hours.

Finally, to those grandparents who step up to care for or raise their grandchildren, especially those with special needs. Your advocacy is worthwhile and appreciated. Do not give up. Yes, it is hard. Yes, you may feel like you are failing. You are not. You may be tired, but you are not failing.

C O N T E N T S

INTRODUCTION

God put great-grandparents Brian and Mary McClellan on a journey with their great-grandson Hunter. Hunter was born hearing impaired, had no heartbeat, and was placed in the NICU for eight days. After Hunter's release, his parents did not follow up with his medical care.

Their journey began when Mary received a call from her daughter Monica, asking Mary to go to her daughter Deb.

This began the journey that led to God stepping in to direct Mary and Brian to begin a journey with Hunter. The journey led them to self-discoveries and discovery of Hunter's other health and emotional issues, including autism.

I hope the reader will see how Hunter soared from a nonverbal and antisocial little boy into an imaginative and extremely social young boy.

It is my wish that this story will touch hearts, that this journey will lead to compassion and bravery—compassion for those who step up to advocate and help not only children but those who are suffering or struggling alone. I hope it gives the courage to fight the good and worthy fight, even when it is complex and often challenging to understand what is happening.

Finally, I hope this book reaches the hearts of all believers. It will open their eyes to understand these families and offer respite.

This book is in the first person, with Mary as the narrator.

The author has changed names to protect identities. Any similarities to individuals, facilities, towns, states, or cities are merely coincidental.

CHAPTER 1

It was a cool but sunny day when my phone rang. It was typical weather for a mid-October month in our state. Mom was busy in her sitting room. We had built a mother-in-law wing in our home. I cleaned and headed to my home office to work when the phone rang. Little did I know that that call would change our lives.

The call was from our eldest daughter, Monica, who lived states away. She was teaching high school English and an AVID class. She had received a call from her daughter, Deb. Deb lives in our state but about four hours away.

The conversation began with "Mom, can you please go to Deb? The police have arrested her husband. Deb and Hunter are upset. I cannot get there to help her."

That is a moment I will never forget. The police had just arrested Deb's husband, Fred, for criminal sexual conduct. Hunter, Deb's son, was frightened. Hunter was twenty-one months old and rightfully frightened by officers cuffing and arresting his father. Of course I agreed to go and help.

Quickly, I picked up the phone to call my husband, Brian, who was at work. "Brian, Monica just called. She asked if I would go and help Deb. I agreed. The police have arrested Fred. Remember, Brian, Deb is not working and is living in a run-down mobile home court. I think we should consider buying food and supplies for her. What do you think?"

Brian replied, "That will be all right. Go, but be safe driving there and back. I think Deb should come live with us. We can help take care of Hunter while she becomes organized."

I replied, "I am going prepared to see if she needs any rent paid too. I will let Mom know and then take off. Love you."

Brian replied, "OK, be careful. Let me know when you get there and when you leave to come home."

"Will do," I replied.

I called my bank and had money transferred from my savings to my checking. Mom was sitting in a chair in her sitting room. I went to inform her that I would be leaving. "Mom, Monica just called. The police just arrested Deb's husband. Monica asked if I would go and help. So I agreed. I will fill you in later. Monica is teaching and cannot arrange to get to Deb quickly enough. I called Brian. He has agreed and is aware that I will be leaving. Be safe. Do not forget to lock your walker."

While driving, I could not help but remember how rough a life Deb had been through. Monica's first marriage was abusive. Her husband had been in the US Marines and then active in the US Marine Corps Reserves. He was a tough guy who thought it perfectly fine to physically and emotionally abuse her: knives between the box springs and mattress; knives throughout the house stuck into the floors, ready to grab; pulling her hair; throwing or slamming her against walls; forcing her to ride her bicycle to work while pregnant even after having been hit by an automobile; and so much more.

One day, Monica called us. She asked us to come and bring her and Deb home during her first husband's duty with the reserves. Deb was three or four months old. Monica did not want her baby to become abused. After we had a discussion, we went and brought her home with us.

As I continued driving, memories and ideas were running through my mind—one thought after another in fragmented order. My thoughts then turned to Deb and her troubled youth. Monica did end up divorcing her first husband, Jack. Initially, the court did not allow Jack visitation with Deb. Then the court allowed Jack supervised visitation. Next, the court allowed Jack unsupervised two-hour visitation every other week. This was to be within the area where we lived. Eventually, Jack obtained the privilege from the court to have Deb every other weekend at his home. Deb experienced and witnessed abuse and neglect before the age of five.

I needed to get my focus back on my driving. However, the thoughts and memories flooded my mind and heart randomly. I was anxious to get to Deb and Hunter.

Once again, my head was spinning with memories and thoughts as I drove. I began to think about Deb's children with her previous relationship. She had a daughter, Annie, and a son, Alden, with Marten. She and Marten lived together yet had not married. They lived together about four years and then separated. At first, Marten and Deb had joint custody of Annie and Alden. They are only a year apart in age.

I arrived at Deb's at about 2:00 p.m. The run-down mobile home court was also a haven for those dealing and taking illicit drugs. There were garbage bags and cigarette butts on her approach steps. Upon entering, I noticed a very cluttered and messy home, including stacks of clothing either not washed or put away and garbage on the counters and the kitchen table. I could smell cigarette smoke. It was evident that Deb had been smoking. She must have stopped smoking when she observed my approach. I am allergic to the smell of cigarette smoke, which Deb was aware of.

I greeted Deb with a hug. She told me that Hunter was taking a nap. We then sat down at her kitchen table. I began to discuss

Fred's arrest. I asked, "Deb, what do you know or have learned about Fred's arrest? Do you know what triggered his arrest?"

Deb replied, "Annie told Marten's girlfriend, Sophia, that Fred had been hurting her. Marten and Sophia then questioned Annie further. Annie explained things that indicated that she had been sexually molested. Then Marten went to the police. He shared what Annie had said happened. The police became involved and questioned Annie. There was enough for further investigation, and they decided to arrest Fred. I do not understand why Marten would not tell me about this first. I'm not sure if I believe this."

"Deb, I am so sorry about all of this. Let us talk about what you need now and in the immediate future. I came prepared to go shopping and get food and supplies for you. What do you need? Do you have any milk? Do you and Hunter have vitamins?"

Deb opened her refrigerator door and showed me that she had two gallons of milk. She stated that she and Hunter had not been taking any vitamins. I explained that it was essential that both she and Hunter take vitamins. I explained it was especially important since she was under so much stress.

Then I asked, "Deb, how about your rent? Is it paid up to date?"

Deb responded that Fred had just paid it. She then explained that they had to pay rent every two weeks. Deb informed me that the rent receipt had not reflected the last payment correctly. She further told me that the office had assured her that they corrected their records.

"Deb, I am going to pay two weeks' rent. Then I am going to do shopping for food and supplies. When I return, I think Hunter will be awake from his nap. I will visit with him. I would like you to think about coming to live with Grandpa and me. You may also consider getting counseling. Then you might also consider getting a job or going back to college. We could support you and Hunter while you do those things or until things settle down. This is all going to take time. Please pray and think about it."

Deb replied, "OK, Grandma. I will."

I first went to the office to pay two weeks' rent. I explained who I was and what Deb had informed me concerning the error in their last rent receipt. The office clerk confirmed that there had been an error and they corrected their records. I then wrote them the check. Next, I went to the nearest store, where I purchased vitamins for both, diapers, wipes, bread, meats, cheese, cereals, potatoes, laundry supplies, dish soap, and a phone card for Deb.

I arrived back at Deb's, took the groceries in, helped put them away, and sat down to ask if Deb had considered our offer. She explained that she felt it necessary to stay around a bit longer. It seemed important to her that she learn more of what might happen. Deb explained that she might move in with her biological father, Jack.

"Deb, just know that the offer is there."

Shortly after our conversation, Hunter woke up from his nap. I could not help feeling sorry for this child, our great-grandson. He was terrified when he saw me. He ran and hid behind the fridge. Quickly, I began to wonder how I might help him find just a little bit of joy. It took silly coaxing, but he finally came out, and we had great fun playing. Hunter would not say goodbye. Instead, he ran to Deb and clung to her. I waved goodbye to them as I entered my car. Deb later told me that he cried when I left and did not want me to leave.

While driving back home, I could not get rid of the image of Hunter hovering and hiding behind the refrigerator. My heart was aching for both my granddaughter and great-grandson. I had just ended a class that described actions one might see in a toddler who may have been sexually abused. Hunter's hiding was one potential characteristic. Although it concerned me a bit, I had not observed him long enough to make any determination.

My mind kept wandering and wondering as I drove back home. I needed to stifle that because traffic was heavy. Factories and schools were shutting down for the day. This was a busy city that

I was driving through. Eventually, I allowed the wondering. *Did we do enough for Deb today? Will she be all right? Will Hunter be OK?*

Deb's mom, Monica, had shared with me that she and her husband had been helping Deb. They gave her money to help with expenses: car repairs, rent, and more. Monica then stated they were done helping Deb. They felt it was time for Deb to make better choices.

My heart simply was not sure that was the right thing for Deb, especially considering what Deb was now facing. This was different. Deb needed help because the police had arrested her husband for criminal sexual conduct. He had been sexually molesting Deb's five-year-old daughter. Deb was not working. She was an emotional wreck.

Sure, Deb and Fred had not budgeted wisely. They lived in a poor and a bit dangerous environment. Really! Is this the time to stop helping and loving on your daughter? *Oh well*, I thought. *We just did what we can right now.* I was wondering what might happen next.

I arrived home safely. It was challenging to fill Mom in on why I had made the trip to help Deb. I simply shared with her that the police had arrested Fred. I did not provide the details of the arrest. I merely stated that Monica had called and asked if we could go to Deb. Mom was upset but did understand our decision. It was vital for me to limit the conversations with my mom. She had a Gladys Kravitz personality. Mom would share too much information with whomever she felt would listen. That usually included a member of our family who was a bit emotionally challenged and untrustworthy.

Monica and Deb filled the next few months with text messages, Facebook messages, and phone calls. They included information about upcoming hearings regarding Fred and parental rights. Deb always told me that the parental rights hearings were strictly about

Fred. She stated that she simply had to attend the hearings. We would learn that she was involved too.

Monica's calls would sometimes include conversations such as: "Mom, you must get Hunter right now! Deb is yelling and fighting with her stepmother, Diana. Hunter is right there listening to all of that. He is seeing all of it. You must get him out of there right now!"

I had replied to Monica that I would call Deb first. I picked up the phone and talked with Deb. "Deb, can you stop talking with Diana?"

Deb replied, "No, I cannot! She keeps talking."

I replied, "Would you be able to take Hunter and go somewhere for a little while?" Deb stated that she could because she had a prescription to pick up. She would do so. Deb later called and let me know that she had returned. She explained that she and Hunter were now upstairs and all right.

Once, Monica called to tell me about a call she had received from Deb: "She called and told me that she was drunk all night."

I asked Monica, "Where was Hunter? Did you ask Deb where he was?"

Monica responded, "Yes, I did. She stated that Hunter was OK because he was asleep." I remember thinking that anything could have happened: a fire or another disaster. If so, Deb sure would not have been able to respond well.

Deb and Hunter had moved out of the run-down mobile home court. They now lived in her father's and stepmother's small, unheated attic. That is where they were living. It was now cold outside. There was no heat in the attic! I finally asked, "Monica, what would have happened if there was an emergency, such as a fire?" I do not recall whether her response was appropriate or not.

On occasion, I would contact Deb to ask her if she had considered taking us up on our offer to move in with us. There was always the answer of not yet. She would explain that she had legal things to take care of. Sometimes Deb would simply state that she wished to be near her first two children. I understood that answer. It seemed reasonable. Later I would learn that there was much more behind that answer. Much more.

Four months had passed since I first went to Deb. So much had happened. I continued to pray. I also had begun to save, print, and file questionable or emotionally unhealthy posts of Deb's. It was becoming important to me. My gut instinct was saying that I might need them sometime. I did not know why. I decided it was essential to save them. It became essential.

Deb had started to see a counselor. Her typical day with Hunter, as Deb explained in one message dated January 22, 2015, at 11:51 a.m., was this:

> I am still in pain stomach wise, BC of the lumps. I missed my appointment today; I overslept. I had a tough time sleeping last BC of the pain. And then I accidentally pushed off instead of snooze on my alarm. So, I rescheduled for Monday. On a typical day here, Hunter and I get up, have breakfast, we watch some cartoons; if Diana isn't already up, then we play eat lunch; he usually cuddles and starts to settle down for his nap, goes down for his nap, then I can make any phone calls I need to make, put in apps, he gets up, get some housework done, play some more, do running if we have any, start dinner, eat dinner, bath, relax, cuddles then bed.

As you might notice, Deb writes in run-on sentences and doesn't always use good grammatical order.

Fred now had another court date for CSC against Deb's daughter, Annie. Court had scheduled the hearing for January 27. Before that, Monica had called and informed me that Fred had been making threats against Deb and Annie. Later I learned that Fred had been talking with a fellow inmate. He was trying to arrange for either Annie or Deb to be killed so they could not testify. My communications with Deb were becoming more intense. This was because Deb was upset. Later, I learned that it also was because she was already in another relationship.

Deb finally reached out and wanted to come up for a weekend visit. She did not have any money, and her vehicle was in poor condition. We said we would come and pick her up. I went by myself and picked them up.

When I arrived, Deb had their suitcase all packed. She went to her car to get Hunter's car seat. I stayed in the tiny vestibule with him. He began to scream and cry because he wanted his mom. I picked Hunter up and held him in my arms. Gently I swayed, with Hunter on my hip. I would point to his mom and say, "There is your mom. She is coming right back. You are coming to visit Grandma and Grandpa." Deb returned and installed the car seat in the car. Hunter and I quietly stood and watched her. Next, she got her suitcase, put it in the trunk, and then put Hunter in the car seat.

Hunter liked riding in the car. He made noises on the four-hour trip home. He loved to imitate sounds. Even though he was born hearing impaired, he enjoyed imitating road sounds. He had failed the hearing test at birth. However, I later learned that his parents had never followed through with his needed testing. Deb would often say, "Oh, he can hear! He just does not listen!" He could indeed hear a little in his right ear. His right ear had a high-frequency loss. I later learned that he could not hear in his left ear.

Hunter immediately loved being at our home. He had lots of room to explore and play. He would open and close doors. Unlike other children that age, he would open the door, peer around the edge, and watch how the hinges worked.

Hunter did not sleep well by himself. He would scream and throw blankets out of the crib. He ended up sleeping with Deb both nights.

It was now Saturday. I had committed to help serve meals to the homeless. It was something that I liked to help with. Deb asked if she could come and help. Of course, I said yes. Brian volunteered to watch Hunter. So off Deb and I went. While driving there, Deb told me, "Grandma, I could not do what you do."

"What's that, Deb?" I replied.

"Work with kids in the nursery or young children. I am not good with young kids. I am good with kids when they are older," said Deb. Instinctively, I knew that what Deb had stated was the truth. Even more than instinctively, I knew it because Deb had lost joint custody of her first two children; she now had only visitation rights.

We arrived at the church. The volunteers had the basics set up. I took in my roaster of pulled pork. Then I introduced Deb to the crew. Deb and I received our instructions of how we were to help. First, we set out the serving utensils, and then we helped serve from the buffet. All my friends liked Deb. Deb was doing great and had a beautiful smile on her face. Deb was busty. She was wearing a revealing and low-cut top. Younger men were present and were eying her up. I felt that she may have been, very subtly, flirting with them.

Driving back to our home, Deb shared that she had fun and enjoyed helping serve the homeless. She stated that she liked doing things like that. I hoped her statement was a sign that she was going to decide to take us up on our offer and come live with us. Sunday, we drove her and Hunter back to their home with her father. Deb had not let us know if she had decided to come to live with us one way or the other.

About one month later, after taking Deb home, I woke up at 5:50 a.m. I woke with tears streaming down my face. I had woken from a dream. Usually, I do not dream. When I do, I do not remember them. This dream had a significant impact on me. I did not want to forget the dream. Immediately, I got up and started to journal my dream. I did not journal everything in this dream, but I remember the parts I did not write in my journal. I will never forget those parts. Journaling, I found myself tearing up. Often, I had to stop and dry my tears. The following is my journaled account of the dream:

Friday, March 13, 2015

Tears are gently streaming down my face, joy flooding my very soul—this was my wake-up call, my alarm clock. I arose, feeling confused and slightly frightened. God had just shown me, given me what may be an answer to my prayers. I will have to mention them later.

Before the tears, there had been this dream: It was a Tuesday evening and time to be at church. Johnny was there. He is autistic, has a quirky personality, and looks to be about ten years old.

Johnny's eyes show, no, they gleam, a depth. A depth of sorrow or lonely acceptance. Yet I get the feeling there is peace.

Moments ago, Johnny was on the floor; a group of boys was mocking him, were kicking, and punching him. I walked up and stopped them. There was nothing significant in the process. It was as if just my presence was enough to cause the bullying to cease.

In this dream, church programs kept in the process: King's kids, Gal time, Guy stuff, and other classes. Johnny and I quietly just walked around. I seemed to have decided to stay close and be his "guard." I asked him if he was ok, and he quietly replied, "Yes." So, we hung together.

Programs were ending, Johnny walked to the stage and sat at the piano. This evening, it was an old-fashioned piano, not an electronic keyboard. Slightly behind him, still not on the stage with him, Johnny began to play the piano. It was just moments of music. Those around, including myself, stopped in quiet amazement and awe at the beauty of the sound and the joy emanating from him. We hear of such things and gifts; now, we share the experience.

He did not play but just moments and rose. I joined Johnny, and somehow Johnny ends up going home with me. Johnny is now part of our family.

It is a Sunday morning, once again, at church, and I am walking through the sanctuary, doing my usual thing: stopping to chat with people before the service. Johnny is walking around, close by but not right by my side. I can see him. He is never out of my eyesight. Merely turning my head, I can see him. This is our pattern.

The worship team is still off somewhere in prayer. Soon beautiful music is playing. I turn, knowing who I will see. There is a mixed response within the sanctuary: Amazement and criticism. Quietly, I walk up to the stage, stand next to Johnny, then sit on the bench next to him. He finishes, we look each other in the eyes. Johnny is smiling. I, too, am smiling while gentle tears stream down my cheeks.

I turn and begin to speak. "Johnny is fearfully and wonderfully made!" I say this to the congregation. Then I turned to Johnny and said: "Johnny, before you were in your mother's womb, God knew you! He fearfully and wonderfully made you be just who you are; you are unique. He loves you, and so do I. Do you know that when the Bible says to fear

God, it means to love Him? Well, then when God fearfully made you, he revered and loved you too."

I looked down to see that someone had given me a mic. Turning to Johnny, I asked, "Do you know how to play O Holy Night?" He said, "Yes." I asked, "Will you play it for us?" Johnny turned and began to play.

In the end, I wrote: "I do not know what Hunter's journey is going to look like. I do not know what our journey with Hunter will look like. This much I do know—that God wants us on that journey."

I do not usually share anything that I journal with Brian. I do not often journal. This time, I did share it with Brian. He read it and merely looked puzzled. He did not know how to react. Weeks later, he shared with me that he had been behind in reading his Daily Bread. He shared that it had said not to be afraid of adoption. Adoption! This was furthest from our minds. We just wanted to help our granddaughter, Deb. We loved her dearly. She had a rough childhood. Yes, she had not been making good decisions. Her heart was good. We were willing to help Deb.

Both Brian and I had been praying about Deb and Hunter. We had changed our offer to Deb about living with us. We still had that option available to her. However, we shared that we would be willing to take temporary custody of Hunter. That way, if this new option allowed her to continue resolving her current issues, she would have more flexibility to accomplish them. Our prayers included that God would help Deb decide to allow us to have temporary custody of Hunter.

I remembered the following from my dream but did not journal: I waited for someone to come and pick Johnny up. When no one did, I simply took him home with us. I also remembered what the comments were as I headed up to the stage: "Where are his parents? Don't they know that he does not belong there?" and

"Isn't he playing beautifully?" I also remember that after I asked Johnny to play "O Holy Night" for us, I turned and headed down the stairs. Tears were streaming down my face. Then I woke, and tears were streaming down my face. There was anger in my heart. I wanted to finish the dream. Yet I knew that God was trying to tell me something. Something significant.

CHAPTER 2

Mary! Remember what happened next! God orchestrated a phone call that you were about to receive. Little did I know that it would be the second phone call that created the more extensive journey with Hunter.

March 18, 2015, I received a telephone call from Deb. This call had happened five days after the dream. Deb asked if we could come and pick up Hunter. She stated that she had just received notice. She was to attend a parental right hearing the next day. I asked her if it regarded her parental rights. She noted that it was regarding Fred's. I then asked her to give me her caseworker's name and phone number. I simply wanted to make sure that it was all right to pick up Hunter. Deb replied, "You do not need to do that. I have full custody of Hunter. It will not be necessary for you to call her." I was convinced that this was not the case. However, I went and picked up Hunter. Hunter traveled well and enjoyed the trip.

When we arrived home, I placed a picture on our buffet of Deb holding Hunter. It was at his eye level so that he could see her all the time. He never missed her. He never cried for her. He was pleased to be back in our home.

We had converted my office, which was next to our bedroom, into a combination office and bedroom. We placed a crib in there. That is where I would put Hunter down for a nap and at night. He still did not like to be in a crib or to sleep alone. Yes, he screamed and cried. We would let him remain upset for a small amount of time. Then we would go in and gently rub his back until he calmed down. We also had a lullaby playing softly. Eventually, he would drift off to sleep.

The next day, after the hearing, I received a phone call from Deb's caseworker, Carrie. She asked me if I had expected her phone call. I told her that I had not but was hoping to receive one. Every child deserves love and protection. That was why I knew that I would provide information about Deb—accurate and complex events regarding Deb.

Carrie told me that the hearing was regarding Deb's parental rights. Carrie continued to inform me that Deb now had "benchmarks" to show that she could "step up to the plate and be a mom." Carrie continued, "You know that I can send the police there right now and have them pick up Hunter?"

I replied, "No, but I was sure hoping that you would call me."

I then began filling Carrie in on the calls from Monica to me regarding what Deb had been doing. In addition, I informed her of Deb's troubled youth. Carrie proceeded to tell me that she was going to have our local CPS workers come and check on Hunter. Carrie had stated that she knew that Hunter was in a safe place. I recall thinking, *Really? How could she?* Of course, she could. All she had to do was to run a background check on us.

Then she stated that she would let Deb and me work out when to return Hunter. He needed to be back for certain appointments. I asked Carrie, "What happens if Deb does not meet those benchmarks?"

Carrie replied, "She will lose Hunter." Carrie also informed me that Hunter's legal representative would need to contact me. He did; his name was Kevin. It so happened that he had relatives who lived in our area. He stated that he would meet Hunter at our home on April 1.

The next day, our local CPS workers showed up. We did not know when they would arrive. Hunter and I had been playing. I had cookies baking. Hunter was laughing and teasing me. He was simply content and happy. They needed to have a tour of our home. It included looking into cabinets, refrigerators, and a freezer. Both workers stated, "Any child would be lucky to grow up here." You see, we had a 4,400-square-foot home with six bedrooms and four bathrooms. The lower level had themed rooms: the Lodge, the Victorian Room, the Captain's Quarters, the Cabin, and the Cave. It was a safe and sturdy home. Hunter had sat down by my feet. He laughed and giggled as the workers said their final goodbyes and "Nice to meet you." They then informed me how often they would come. They could not help but notice how happy Hunter was.

I called Deb and informed her of Kevin's call. Deb replied, "Oh, I thought I told you. I have appointments for Hunter on April 1." She had not informed me of this.

After church, we communicated further. "Deb, Hunter loves church. He always says, 'Yay,' when we head for the nursery." Deb replied that it would be all right to return Hunter the following Sunday, March 29. Then I informed Kevin of that decision. Kevin said he would meet us at a specific governmental building. The building happened to be about five minutes away from Deb's father's home. I called Deb to tell her that Kevin would meet us first. We would arrive about 3:00 p.m. She agreed and asked me to call Diana when we were on the way.

During Hunter's time with us, we would go outside to play in the snow. Deb had stated that Hunter did not like the snow. She said he was afraid of the snow. One warmer, sunny yet cold, snowy day, Hunter and I went outside to play. The woods had a fresh blanket of wet snow. I said to Hunter, "Let's get our coats and boots and go outside." Hunter quickly went to get his winter clothing on. Brian and I had purchased a coat, gloves, and boots for Hunter.

Hunter and I walked the driveway. Suddenly, Hunter stopped and lifted his head up to the sky. He was in awe of the height of the trees and continued to stare at the treetops. A small gust of wind came up and caused the tops to sway ever so gently. Hunter's face broke into a gigantic smile.

I noticed Hunter's amazed look and said, "Hunter, God made everything. He created and made these amazing trees. It is so beautiful to watch them move." Hunter simply smiled more and clapped his gloved hands in pure delight. He was not accustomed to playing outside.

Sunday, March 29, was a wonderful day at church. We had a nice ride to meet Kevin. We called him and told him that we had arrived. We waited in the car for ten to fifteen minutes. When Kevin arrived, he simply came over, introduced himself, quickly investigated the car, and then said, "He looks great! Everything is good. Goodbye." I recall shaking my head in disbelief. This was a bad check.

I then picked up the phone and called Diana. Diana did not answer. I left a message that we were on our way and would arrive in about five minutes. We arrived around 2:45 p.m. Hunter and I went with a suitcase in hand and knocked on the door. There was no answer. On the door was Carrie's business card. She had come calling, and no one was home, or they did not answer the door. I could hear the vacuum running. I knocked again. Once again, I tried calling Diana. Diana came to the door and greeted us. I did not see Deb. "Diana," I said, "where is Deb?"

Diana replied, "I don't know."

"Diana, could she be upstairs and did not hear us?" Diana opened the door to the upstairs attic. The stairwell was narrow, I could see multiple areas of clothing and garbage on the stairwell. It was an unsafe area. The house reeked of cigarettes. I noticed that there were unemptied ashtrays.

Diana called up the stairs to Deb. There was no response. She motioned for us to sit. Hunter sat in my lap. He did not seem to want to be there. He cuddled in closely with me. Diana then called Jack, Deb's dad. Deb had been with him. When they arrived, Deb's first words were, "I thought you were going to be here at three o'clock."

I replied, "We said about three o'clock. That means we could arrive a bit before or a bit after."

She had not even greeted Hunter. Hunter still did not seem to want to be there. Nor did he greet or reach out to her. Deb approached us and knelt in front of Hunter and me.

Deb began to tell me that she had a job. "Grandma, I got a job starting Monday!"

"That's great, Deb," I replied. "What kind of job?"

Deb replied, "I will be driving a taxi at night. I will have a fifteen-hour shift."

I asked, "Deb, who will babysit Hunter? Will you be able to take him to his appointments?"

Deb replied, "Oh, I will not need a babysitter! I will be working at night." Deb's reply surprised me.

I turned and looked at Diana. "What about you, Diana? Could you watch Hunter?"

Diana replied, "I think I will be starting a new job Tuesday. I just had a good interview. I am sure that I will be working."

Then I turned and looked at Jack. "Jack, what about you, Grandpa? Will you watch Hunter?"

Jack replied, "I will not be able to. I will be having surgery on Tuesday."

I next turned to Deb. "Deb, someone has to watch Hunter while you are at work." Deb stated that she could have her best friend watch him. Deb could drop Hunter off there. Inside, I was cringing! This was an individual who had her children taken away from her. I knew that I would have to leave Hunter there with them. I knew that it was my legal responsibility to do so. I hated it. Deb finally did greet Hunter. It took him about two minutes to respond. It was just a quick hug, and he remained on my lap. I had to leave him. I put Hunter down and explained that we would see him later. Then we said goodbye and left. Immediately, I contacted Kevin. He told me to let Carrie know.

It was two days later that I heard from Carrie. Then another two days later, we received a call from Deb. CPS had advised Deb to call us and see if we were willing to get Hunter. During the phone call, I could hear a man's voice. It sounded like he was giving her guidance in conversation. The conversation went like this: "Grandma, they asked me if I thought that you and Grandpa would be willing to get Hunter. Would you be willing to take him?"

I replied, "Yes, we can do that. I have a doctor's appointment tomorrow morning. We could come after that appointment."

Deb replied, "Thank you. Will you be willing to meet at the courthouse? We can fill out a petition for guardianship. Or do a power of attorney?" I replied that we would be willing to be guardians.

I continue now with my thoughts today. I had been reflecting on what had gone on up to that point. Do you see, Mary? Do you see and understand? God has you on this journey for Hunter's sake. God will reveal what you must learn. I am beginning to feel that my trust is not solely in God. Yet God is going to teach me more.

We scheduled to pick up Hunter on April 2, 2015. I was extremely apprehensive about what that day would look like. During the next couple of days, my mind began to think of Deb, especially about what her personality was like and the things she dealt with as a child.

CHAPTER 3

Deb was a bit of a rebel and had been for years. I will expand on that fact later—just a bit of her history to follow. After Monica first left her husband, Jack, we brought her and Deb to our home. Monica sought and received counseling from our church. The pastor advised Monica to not return to her husband unless he had completed counseling.

We were hopeful that Monica would consider the pastor's advice. However, Monica continued to communicate with her husband. Monica decided to go back before Jack had completed counseling. It was at that point that we set boundaries and guidelines. They were tough, but they had to be. We were aware that Monica had previously called the police when abused. Yet she would always back down and not press charges.

This became our position: "Monica, if you go back, we will not take you back to him. Jack will have to take you back. We will not come to get you again unless you have contacted the police or Women's Resource Center and are serious about leaving. Then we will come and pick you up. However, you will have to commit to stay and follow through." That stance was another of the hardest things that we had to do. However, it was so important. It was tough love.

That day did come. Deb was just months old. Monica's husband had left for his term in the Marine Reserves. Jack's violence had escalated. Monica was now seriously concerned for Deb's safety going forward. First, Monica contacted her friends, who helped pack her and Deb's belongings. Then Monica contacted her pastor. She then had conversations with her pastor. Her pastor also called and talked with me. He stated that Monica was doing the right thing. However, he did not make the same remarks to the legal teams during divorce procedures. When Monica made the call to me, she brought me up to date with what had happened. She then asked if we could get her and Deb.

I will never forget the day I went to pick her up. As I walked through their home, I saw knives between the bedsprings and mattress, stuck in the floor in their bedroom, stuck into their bathroom floor, and (it is a little hazy right now) I believe in the living room floor. It made my skin crawl. Monica had shared that Jack stated he would not tolerate any child or toddler doing … "Or he would slap them against the wall." Monica knew all too well what that was like and what it could do to a child. So she chose to come home.

Once home, Monica signed up for college classes in business administration. She also began divorce proceedings. We paid for her divorce. We stipulated that she would have to finish school and follow through with the divorce. If she did not, then Monica would have to repay us. Initially, the court did not allow Jack any visitation with Deb. Next, the court granted Jack supervised visits. His supervised visits were to be at a location outside of our home.

Eventually, the court allowed Jack to have two-hour-long unsupervised visits every other weekend in our area. On one visit, Jack said they were going to a park. Deb was about two years old. Later, Monica was changing Deb. She saw that Deb's vaginal area was very inflamed and swollen. Monica took Deb to the ER. Upon examination, the doctors stated that they often saw this type of injury when a toddler had fallen, specifically on the seat of a tricycle. Well, we did not have a tricycle for Deb. It would have been impossible for that to have been the cause of her inflamed vaginal area. We all were sure that Jack had molested Deb.

However, there was not enough proof to press charges. The court did not deny Jack's unsupervised visit. The next time Jack came, Deb ran and hid behind a chair. Deb's little fingers were gripping the chair. I can still visualize her tiny fingers gripping the chair. We gently came to Deb and said it was time to visit with her dad. She did leave with him. Yet I could sense her fear. I hated having to allow her to go. Legally, that was precisely what we had to do.

Monica continued her college classes, obtained her associate degree in office administration, and then obtained a position with a highly reputable hospital in the pediatric intensive care unit. As Monica's confidence and healing grew, she began to date. We were not sure about her choice of her next husband. I wondered if this young man was a wise choice. His name was Butch. He had an excellent job in a factory. He had been working there for two to three years.

I became more concerned when Monica shared that Butch had abused drugs, had now been clean since age twenty, and now helped on the NARC team. She felt that made him a safe and desirable choice. I thought she simply wanted to be married and on her own. Of course, she also felt that Butch was genuinely in love with her. I had my doubts and concerns. We did not attend their marriage. They decided to have their wedding in another state. Butch's extended family lived in the area and could attend.

Deb was three years old when Monica remarried. Deb now had to live in another home, a home that did not include us there with her for support. This had to be traumatic for her. She had been with us since she was just months old. We sure did miss her. Deb was always gentle, happy, and an average toddler while in our safe and secure home. Her environment was soon to change.

Now Deb had unsupervised visits with her biological father every two weeks. Plus, she was getting to know her stepfather, Butch.

After Monica, Deb, and Butch moved into their own home, we did not see them often. They both were working and now lived a little farther away. Both Brian and I were working full-time. We both had jobs that often required working overtime. Communications were usually a quick phone call or two, filling us in on things happening. Usually, Monica would call and report things that caused them distress.

Deb's unsupervised visits with Jack were now for the whole weekend. Jack lived in a rough neighborhood. I recall Monica calling me after one visit. Deb was about four. Deb had returned home quite upset. She had been outside playing. Suddenly, she watched an individual kill another. It happened just across the street from Jack's home. It was a terrifying experience for Deb. Monica was rightfully upset and angry that the incident had occurred. Yet Jack still did not lose his visitation rights. We felt blessed that Deb had not been shot.

Deb's visits with Jack often did not go well: stepmothers who did not treat her well, animals that injured her slightly. I cannot even imagine how confused a child's mind must be. Fear? Acceptance? Is it just the norm?

One day, Monica called to report that Deb's biological father had accused Butch of molesting Deb. Deb was about five years old at that time. CPS initiated an investigation. The investigation could not definitively prove the complaint. Officials could not file a case against Butch.

CHAPTER 4

It is time to reflect on April 2, 2015, the day we arrived to pick up Hunter—the day that Deb and I completed the petition for guardianship of Hunter.

We arrived and parked. Deb was already in the parking lot. We all left our vehicles and proceeded to the courthouse. Hunter held Deb's hand as we crossed the street. We all walked to the clerk's office to request and complete the petition for guardianship. Together, Deb and I were completing the petition. Brian and Hunter quietly played together across the room. I remember that Deb had to select the reasons or goals for the petitioning for guardianship. One benchmark was "to take parenting classes." I asked Deb, "How about choosing this?"

Angrily, she replied, "I do not need to take parenting classes. It is none of their business! They are too nosy!"

I said, "But, Deb, don't you think that it is important to make sure that children are safe? Wouldn't you want all children to be safe?"

Deb simply replied, "They are too nosy."

Once Deb and I completed the petition, it was time to pay the clerk. We offered to pay the fee. Deb refused and paid for the petition. She had only been working for about two weeks. I realized that it must have put a financial burden on her. Then we offered to at least pay half of the fee. Still, Deb insisted on paying. We all received a copy of the completed petition. When finished, we headed back to the parking lot. Deb got Hunter's suitcase and car seat. She put the car seat in and said goodbye to Hunter. She said, "Bye. Mommy loves you." We buckled Hunter in.

We all headed to our own homes. When we had turned onto the last road home, Hunter recognized the sound. He started getting excited. Hunter could only speak about five to ten words like: thank you (tank oo), mama, hi, and bye. Hunter once again rode well.

That evening, Hunter began screaming and crying while he was sleeping. I went in to see what was wrong. It was a bit strange. Hunter had his eyes closed like he was asleep. Yet he was slapping his legs, screaming and crying. I picked him up to comfort him. I kept thinking, *What did they do to you?* Deb had a pet snake and pet rats. Diana and Jack allowed those animals to be downstairs. However, they did not let Hunter play downstairs unless supervised by Deb. I will never know what happened to Hunter. There could have been mice in the attic. If so, had they crawled on Hunter? I do not know. I was able to comfort him. He fell asleep and slept well the remainder of the night.

He was also a very fussy eater. He was a very OCD eater. We supplemented with PediaSure. He would eat toast. We could put butter on it, but we could not cut it. First, he would eat all around the crust. Then he would finish eating it. He also ate waffles. Hunter also ate them in a pattern. First, he ate around the waffle edge. Then he would tear off the ridges and eat them. Finally, he would pick up the waffle and finish eating it. Only occasionally could we get him to eat scrambled eggs or spaghetti. Taking him anywhere to eat could be a challenge. Later, we would learn that this resulted from being on the spectrum and having sensory issues.

I had made an appointment with a pediatrician for Hunter just before we left to pick him up. So on April 8, Hunter was in to see Dr. Kelly. Dr. Kelly saw both adults and children. He was also our family doctor. Dr. Kelly was amazed at how small Hunter was for twenty-seven months. I remember what Hunter was doing when the doctor walked into the examining room. Hunter was spinning the doctor's chair, looking underneath as it turned around, watching the components working. Dr. Kelly did a quick chuckle and stated that Hunter might just become an engineer. The doctor wasted no time referring Hunter to a speech therapist and an ear, nose, throat specialist.

Speech therapy was on April 14. That visit included an assessment of where Hunter was developmentally in that area. The assessment resulted in diagnosing Hunter as severely delayed. The ENT appointment with Dr. Eric was on April 20. Tests indicated that Hunter was not hearing in his left ear. Dr. Eric then scheduled Hunter for tubes to be put into his ears and a sedated ABR (automated brain response) test. The doctor's office staff scheduled the procedures for May 21, 2015, at 8:15 a.m.

I informed Deb about the surgery and schedule. We had not yet had our hearing for the guardianship. The court scheduled our guardianship hearing for May 7, 2015. If the judge were to deny our guardianship, we might have to obtain Deb's signature of approval for his surgery. I informed Deb that we might need her signature. She understood and agreed that she would sign if needed. She wanted to be there for the surgery. I informed her that we all had to be at the hospital at 5:00 a.m. the day of surgery. She did not think that she could make it with her new job. We agreed to text her when he was out of surgery.

Deb did call and talk with Hunter on April 16. I had to keep the phone on speaker so he could respond. Hunter liked to walk while he listened on the phone. He did not talk much, but he loved to be on the phone. That was one of his favorite forms of pretend playing, which he did often. I imagined that he was modeling how Deb talked on a phone.

Backing up a bit, Easter fell on April 5 that year. We had purchased a little suit for Hunter. We also purchased new toys for him. One was a little car that he could ride in the house. Our great room was thirty-two feet by thirty-two feet. The great room consisted of a dining area, kitchen, and living room. It had a large kitchen island. The island was off center within our great room. Hunter would ride his car around and around. He was so happy. Hunter would also chase me around the island. Sometimes, I let Hunter think he caught me. Our lives were full of laughter. Other times, he and I would sit and scoot all around the island.

Shortly after Hunter's surgery, I received a phone call from Deb's county's director of their Early On program. She informed me that Deb had not complied with the required Early On program. The director then stated that Deb was difficult to get a response from. In addition, they had notified our county's director of their Early On program. The director informed me that we had to enroll Hunter in the Early On program. I had no idea what that consisted of. It did not intimidate me. It was something that I was willing to comply with, learn, and understand. I did receive the call and provided them with our information. Our first Early On appointment was on May 18.

Our church's teen group put on a musical program on April 24. We took Hunter to that event. He sat on our lap. We had an up-front table seat. The program was fantastic! I was wondering how he would react to all the different sounds. No problem! Not only did Hunter enjoy it, but he was also well behaved.

At one point, Hunter looked at a gentleman at the following table. Suddenly, Hunter was reaching out to him. That was unusual for Hunter. He usually would stay close to Brian or me. However, the gentleman allowed Hunter to come and sit with him. They were such a lovely family. Our church family was impressed with how well behaved Hunter was.

We knew that Hunter had been in an environment that included domestic violence and episodes of anger. We knew that there were and would always be things Hunter experienced of which we would never learn. It was essential to show Hunter love, give him a sense of security, and accept that an accidental drop of a toy or something was all right. So after fifty years of marriage, we began to group hug when Brian went to work. We also began to say, "Uh oh, spaghetti o's! Try again." We would say this when he accidentally dropped a toy or something else. This helped Hunter to feel secure and helped him to be calm. When he was anxious or afraid, it was only then that he would scream, kick, slap, or flap his hands.

Between this time and the May 7 petition to guardianship hearing, I took Mom for labs, a heart scan, and eye appointments. We managed to do all of this with Hunter present. He was always well behaved, even though he was continually active.

It was now May 7 and time to travel downstate to the courthouse. Our guardianship hearing was at 10:30 a.m. We had to leave about 6:30 a.m. Still, Hunter traveled well. He was still in diapers. We made pitstops to change Hunter.

Deb had not yet arrived. We checked in with the clerk and headed up to the courtroom floor to attend our guardianship hearing. The county had assigned Deb a new caseworker because she now lived in a different county, different from the county she lived in with Fred. Her caseworker, Kenneth, arrived. He had to meet with Deb first. He waited in one area, and we waited outside, in the hall of the courtroom.

When I headed to the restroom to change Hunter, Deb arrived. She saw us and said that she wanted to change him. Hunter easily went to her. She changed Hunter, and we proceeded back to the courtroom.

Kenneth saw us and needed to speak with Deb. After Kenneth and Deb met, Hunter and I joined them and walked toward Brian. Kenneth remarked that someone might have to go to jail. Neither Deb nor I heard his full remark. However, Deb quickly turned and, frightened, asked, "Am I going to have to go to jail?"

Kenneth replied, "No. Someone else."

Deb then replied, "OK." I could tell that Deb was frightened. About four or five months later, Kenneth let me know that Deb had plead guilty to all but one of the six or seven of the seven or eight charges. This was the first time that I became aware of charges against Deb. Not until then had he shared this with me.

Hunter sat on Deb's lap as we waited inside the courtroom for our turn in front of the judge. This day, she also chose to wear a too-revealing top. Hunter reached up to play with Deb's breasts. She quickly moved his hand. She had never nursed him, so I found that to be strange. The judge reviewed the paperwork, asked a couple of simple questions, and granted the guardianship. He then directed us to go to the clerk's office and receive the papers.

When we arrived in the clerk's office, the clerk came up to the counter and reviewed the papers. She then explained to Deb that we would now be making all decisions regarding Hunter. However, we could mutually choose to do so together. The clerk then looked at me and said, "I am extremely familiar with this case. I am sure that I will transfer this case to your county soon." Then, looking at Deb, the clerk said, "You may not make any decisions for him. They are his parents now." Deb was standing behind me. I could not see her face. My heart broke! This was my granddaughter. I loved her. We still had the mindset that we were stepping up to help her until things settled down for her. I hurt knowing that her heart indeed must have been hurting by the clerk's remarks. The clerk's remark about us being his parents was not legally correct. Her statements were unkind.

We received our copies of the completed guardianship papers. Then we asked Deb if she would like to have lunch with us somewhere, go to a park, or get ice cream before we left again. That would give her time with Hunter. She said yes.

First, we went to a park. She and Hunter walked hand in hand to the playground equipment. Hunter began to climb up and slide down. Once, she sat at the top of one of the smaller slides.

Deb simply quietly sat there, her head slightly bowed down. I understood that she was sad.

As she did so, Hunter continued to play. Then we went to an ice-cream shop. Hunter ate ice cream. That made it easier to spend time together. The shop had picnic tables under a tree at the back of the shop. We proceeded to the table and had our ice cream. Then Deb and Hunter walked a little ways away. She chose an area to lie down on the ground. Hunter sat beside her. They played gently.

Soon, it was time to leave. Deb walked Hunter over to the car and put Hunter into his seat. Then she asked if it would be all right to bring someone with her when she visited. We wondered if it was a male. She replied, "Yes, but he wouldn't be staying in the same room with me." We replied that we did not think that was a good idea. We also stated that her visits were to allow time for her and Hunter to continue their bond. So, no. Not yet. As Deb said her last goodbye to Hunter, he began to cry. He did not want her to leave. He stopped crying within thirty seconds after we left. Hunter continued to be OK and happy. Deb later shared that she had cried all the way home. My heart hurt for her. It was May 15 when Deb called again to talk with Hunter.

CHAPTER 5

Next up was surgery day. We arrived early. The surgery day was long. Poor Hunter, he was very apprehensive. We were already aware that he was reluctant to be with anyone other than Brian or me. The team was great. I had to laugh at one of the nurse assistants. He was a tall and stout man. In addition to his surgical attire, he had also put on a red clown's nose. He was trying to be a Patch Adams. Hunter was afraid of him. I held Hunter to help comfort him.

After the procedures, Dr. Noah from the hearing clinic explained the results. He stated that Hunter would require a hearing aid in his right ear. The doctor did not believe a hearing aid would benefit his left ear. At least not yet. They stated that he could only hear loud sounds like an airplane or motors. We filled Deb in on the results and the upcoming scheduled appointments.

Her next call was to me on May 30. She wanted to ask me if I knew what was wrong with her thigh. I do not remember what her thigh complaint was. Her call seemed strange.

Our days now began to be terribly busy: Early On appointments, Mom's appointments with specialists, Hunter's appointments with specialists, and everyday routines, including cleaning, cooking, trying to potty train, trying to adjust Hunter to sleeping alone, haircuts, and all the regular play and teaching one usually does with a toddler. I remember one of the first attempts to potty train Hunter. I sat him on the chair and waited. He had not been successful. When I got Hunter off the chair, he turned and faced the bathroom toilet and peed!

Hunter had anxieties when he arrived. Hunter's biggest anxiety was separation from either Brian or me. Hunter's separation anxieties interfered with therapies and appointments. He did well with the Early On sessions only if I was present. Hunter was learning more words. However, he was unable to enunciate them correctly. During the Early On sessions, I often interpreted. He could now say more words, like the following: outside (oubide), love you (lub oo), and more.

Monica finished teaching for the year. She and Deb had arrived to spend about three days visiting Hunter and us. They were to arrive on June 22. Monica arrived first. Deb wanted to take Hunter to the beach. Deb desired to get a tan. Hunter still slept in his room next to us. Deb slept downstairs in the Cabin.

The next day, Hunter had woken early. We played while Deb was still sleeping. Monica and Hunter played a bit too. Deb still had not woken up. Deb woke up a little after noon. Hunter had played hard. He was getting tired and hungry. I fed Hunter an early lunch. Then I put him down for his nap.

Deb was not happy that he was sleeping. The weathercaster had issued a high-wind warning and was not recommending people to swim in the lakes that day. Even though unhappy, Deb calmed down and accepted that fact.

The next day, Deb woke up at 11:00 a.m. Unfortunately, Hunter had woken up early again. Only this time, he wanted to play outside. Hunter and I went out, and I pulled him around and around in his wagon. We went all around the large driveway circle. We also raced each other around the driveway circle. He got tired and went down for a nap early again, even before having lunch.

Deb was furious. Monica and I explained that Hunter had gotten up early and played hard. Then Deb asked where the nearest store was. She wanted to get tanning lotion, as she had forgotten hers. I explained that Hunter would be waking soon, the weather was good, and we could go to the beach. However, she would not have time to get her tanning lotion and get back in time. After further explanation, Deb accepted the fact.

It was interesting at the beach. Deb did take Hunter's hand and walked him out into the water once. Monica and I simply stayed close to the shore. We watched Deb and Hunter interact. Shortly, Deb brought Hunter back to the beach. What impressed me the most was that Monica spent the time playing with Hunter. Deb sat near and did not interact with Hunter. I watched as Deb swirled her hands in the sand, head bent down as she sat on the beach, occasionally looking at a stone she found, not interacting with Hunter. Monica was not incredibly pleased with how Deb acted.

We were all up, getting ready for the day. Deb was downstairs getting ready to leave. I was beginning to get Hunter's breakfast, and Mom was getting ready for her doctor's appointment that day. Deb came up the stairs with her suitcase. Hunter realized that she was going to leave. My heart aches, even now, as I write what happened next. It is something that will live with me forever. Hunter began to cry and scream. He began to repeatedly yell words that I had not heard him say, "No, Mama!" as Hunter was reaching for her. He did not want her to leave. Never had he looked at the picture of Deb and himself and reacted. Yet today, he was distraught! Monica saw Hunter's reaction. Monica and Deb had planned to leave together on the twenty-fifth. Monica decided to leave before Deb left. Monica did not want to chance that their leaving at the same time might cause Hunter to become even more upset. Deb hurried out when she left. Later she told me that she had cried all the way home.

I was now with a terribly upset Hunter. I was still trying to get us ready to take Mom to her appointments. As hard as I fought it, the tears came. I did my best to hide them. I had not yet finished making the pancakes. Hunter came up beside me, grabbed my hand, and squeezed it hard. I looked down at Hunter and said, "Grandma is right here, and Grandma is not going to leave."

I remember feeling so sorry for all children, especially those within the foster system; they indeed must have to go through this trauma. Oh, how my heart ached. We did get to Mom's doctor's appointment. It was our practice to go out to eat after her appointments. That day, we went to Cracker Barrel. I was fighting not to cry. I was so sad.

The next thing Hunter did was beautifully amazing. We always listened to the ABC song together. Sometimes I would sing it. I always encouraged Hunter to sing along. He usually would only do it by himself. If I sang, he would only listen. Hunter, right there in Cracker Barrel, put my face in his one hand and turned my head, nose next to his. Then I heard Hunter humming. I recognized that he was humming the ABC song. So I began to sing softly while he was humming. He never stopped humming this time.

I thought that Hunter had finished. I began to turn away. Hunter moved my face back, nose to nose again. Once again, he hummed, and I softly sang right there in Cracker Barrel. It was as if he knew that I was sad and he wanted to make me feel better. That was the last time Hunter called her "Mom."

The following month of July was again busy: appointments for Mom and Hunter, Early On sessions and events, plus our annual weekend McClellan family get-together. Hunter's type of play consisted of playing with his new toys, lining up his cars (part of his OCD behavior), and spinning his body. Hunter had two different methods of spinning: sitting on the floor and moving his body in circles, or he would stand, with his head slightly facing the floor, while twirling his body in circles. Sometimes he would also extend his arms outward at his sides in the standing position when circling. I did not consider, or even realize, that what Hunter was doing was because he might be on the spectrum. It was not until later that I learned what "stimming" was. So when our annual weekend family get-together happened, I had no idea how Hunter's behaviors would impact those who attended.

We always held the weekend get-together at our home. This was the first one with Hunter there. This was quite a weekend of firsts! Hunter immediately came to me each time anyone arrived. He was highly apprehensive about each person.

Often, I held Hunter while trying to visit or organize our meals and events. It was, indeed, awkward for me. I am sure that it left two of our family members feeling a bit uncomfortable. Yet we did have an enjoyable time. However, I often had to separate myself from the activities and our family guests.

I recall our son, Colton, telling me that he thought we were too old to care for Hunter. I chuckled as I just typed that statement. I was a highly active sixty-seven-year-old lady then. A little later, our sister-in-law, Lydia, said, "Mary, you should find a young family in your church that could adopt Hunter." I replied that I thought it might have to come to something like that. Brian and I still wanted our granddaughter, Deb, to live with us. Adoption, by anyone, was the furthest thing from either of our minds.

Before going to the beach, Hunter had begun to get tired. He was thirty months old and still taking naps. He had only been with us full-time for three months. The number of people and activities was overwhelming for Hunter. I had to take him into our bedroom and lie down with him. Eventually, he drifted off to sleep. I was able to put him down for a quick nap and visit.

One of our weekend events was spending time at the beach. We usually did this in the late afternoon. We all headed there at various times. That day, family members had left first. Hunter and I joined them later. When Hunter and I arrived, our son, Colton, was sitting on the beach. He and his girlfriend, Julie, had beach chairs. They were sitting there watching Hunter and me play in the water. When Hunter and I came out, Colton said, "Mom, I could not do what you did."

"What, Colton?" I replied.

Colton said, "Play that way in the water with a young child."

I simply smiled and said, "That was easy."

The weekend ended with our nephew, Lee, taking a group picture of all of us together outside. It is a picture that I treasure. However, this was our second annual family get-together. Monica did not join us at this event. She did not come because she had to get back to get ready for her new teaching position.

I remember an overwhelming sense of sadness during our guardianship, wondering what would happen. The judicial system had not yet sentenced Fred and sent him to prison. Deb would call occasionally and fill me in on the events happening regarding his trial.

One time, Deb shared that she had visited Fred in jail. Fred had informed Deb that one of his jail mates had made serious threats—threats about killing Annie so she could not testify. Deb shared that information with the jail guards or other authorities. Deb stated that the authorities had not done anything about the threats.

August 2015 was busy for our family. We spent time with speech therapy for Hunter, calls from Deb, a dental appointment and a doctor's appointment for Hunter, and a weekend visit from our nephew Dexter and his family. It happened to be a weekend that Deb planned to come for a visit too.

We were in the beginning stages of speech therapy for Hunter. Hunter's anxieties kept him from being successful in his therapy visits. While we waited, I often gave Hunter piggyback rides until it was time for therapy. The receptionists always watched us. Sometimes they looked down to answer a phone call or check in the next patient. They always had smiles on their faces while watching me give Hunter those piggyback rides. It was strange. At least I think it must have looked odd to others as they watched me give Hunter those piggyback rides.

The piggyback rides were merely a method to keep him from crying, screaming, or spinning on the floor. The therapy sessions were not easy at first. Hunter often would not or could not make the sounds they were working on with him. It took time for Hunter to learn to trust our therapist. Oh, she was such a great therapist. She was so patient and exceedingly kind.

One of Deb's calls was again to ask if she could bring someone with her on her visit on the weekend of the fifteenth. I replied that I still did not feel that was wise. Her visits should be her time to bond with Hunter. She asked, "What about bringing his cousins with me sometime?" I again said no. I called both of Deb's caseworkers regarding Deb's requests. Both Carrie and Kenneth stated that Deb and Hunter's time was to bond. It was not our decision alone. I am sure that Deb and Monica both felt that it was. However, that was not the case.

Dexter and his family were already at our home when Deb arrived. Hunter had been playing with his young cousins. We were out on the back deck. They played in the little pool and with small cars and trucks. We coaxed Hunter to say hi to Deb. He was reluctant but did go say hi to Deb. He also allowed Deb to pick him up and give him a quick hug. We decided to go to a beach and let the kids play in the water. Deb was on her phone more than anything. At one point, I heard Deb say to whomever she was talking, "I am stuck here in the middle of nowhere!"

Dexter and his wife, Mandy, noticed that Deb was not attempting to go into the water with Hunter, not even to wade. It took coaxing from us to get Deb to do that with Hunter. She finally did but quickly and only once. I was usually the one in the water with Hunter.

Sunday morning, Hunter, Brian, and I were getting ready for church. Deb was getting ready to leave for her home. I asked Hunter to say goodbye to his mom. "Hunter, won't you say goodbye to your mom before we go to church?"

Hunter emphatically stated, "No!"

I then took Hunter to Deb and said, "Say goodbye to your mom."

Again, he screamed, "No!"

Deb replied, "Fine! Just be a brat!"

Early On appointments were in our home. They went well. Hunter still could not enunciate clearly the unfamiliar words. His right hearing aid had come in. However, it was not correct. The hearing clinic then loaned one to Hunter until his corrected device arrived. It arrived on September 2. I simply continued working on speech with Hunter. The speech therapist did as well. We were making baby steps in getting Hunter to learn and say unfamiliar words.

I still had my mother to take care of mixed in with these events. She had to see her heart specialist more often. I took her to appointments to get her hair done. Plus, I did all the house cleaning—even in her wing.

I had noticed a large bump behind each of Hunter's ears. I made an appointment for Hunter to see his doctor. Dr. Kelly was not available. We were able to see Dr. Steel. He was so good with Hunter. Dr. Steel was concerned and ordered an ultrasound of his head. Hunter had two smaller cyst-like bumps that the doctor felt we should watch. We were to go back if there was any change in size. So far, six years later, they are still the same size.

In August 2015, Deb informed me that she had a boyfriend. I said, "Deb, has he ever been in trouble with the law?"

She replied, "Oh wow! I do not know—a speeding ticket when he was in high school. He is close to his family. He is a nice guy. He went with me to one of Fred's hearings." I did not pursue that topic any longer.

Deb could get irritated quickly. I should have been more subtle when I asked about him. She had had anger issues since she was a young girl. I knew that Marten, the biological father of Annie and Alden, had met this young man. His name was Maxton. One day I asked Marten, "What kind of guy is Maxton?"

Marten replied, "I do not know. He seemed all right the few moments that we saw him. When we met at the park, he was with Deb for her visit with Annie and Alden."

Marten told Deb that I had asked him what he thought of Maxton. Well, that set off a trigger for her! She called me at 6:10 p.m. on October 15 and wanted to know why I had asked Marten about her boyfriend. I replied, "Deb, I simply wanted an objective opinion. One from someone other than you. It is no big deal. We care about you and your safety. You married Fred, even though you knew he had been in prison. He was there because he committed an armed robbery in a drug lord community. You do not always think things through. I wanted to know that you would be in a safe relationship."

Deb called me on September 17, 2015, at 7:40 p.m. She was sobbing and asking me to do her a favor. I stated that I would if I could. She then told me that I could because I knew how to pray. Her previous manager at ICab, John, had tried to commit suicide. John was in the ICU, and no one could see him except his immediate family. I prayed over the phone with her. She never once asked about Hunter. She did inform me that she was still doing home health care. A sidenote here: ICab fired Deb.

Fred had his pretrial hearing on September 27, 2015. I learned that Alden also said that Fred had "hurt him" too. The police had investigated Alden's claim before Fred's hearing. Alden's claim was insufficient to bring charges against Fred. At that hearing, the judge terminated Fred's parental right. Deb had informed me that Fred had told the judge that Deb was a "bad mom." Fred stated he wanted Hunter to live with Deb's grandparents, which, of course, was his reference to us. He knew that we had offered to take temporary custody of Hunter.

October was a busy and average month. Hunter still passed by the picture of Deb and him. He did not stop to look at it. Hunter never acted like he missed Deb—except briefly after the guardianship determination hearing and then significantly when she left after her visit in June.

Hunter also continued in speech therapy sessions and Early On sessions. The speech therapy sessions and our tutoring

Hunter had begun to increase his vocabulary. His enunciation continued to be extremely poor. The high-frequency sounds, especially the following letters and letter blends—th, c, s, and f—were difficult for him to say. In addition, he could not enunciate the ending sounds of most words.

The Early On group suggested that I make a memory book for Hunter, one in which I was to include pictures of his favorite toys, activities, or other known items. They wished for us and them to use this as a tool to encourage more language. I thought it only fair also to include a picture of his mom. That created a surprising and upsetting reaction from Hunter. I began to share the memory book with Hunter. The first picture was of his little red tricycle, the next was another favorite item, and the third was a picture of his mom. Hunter grabbed that book and screamed, "No!" Then, he violently threw the memory book down. He refused to look at it. I contacted Early On and informed them of Hunter's reaction. They suggested that I put the book away. They felt it caused trauma to Hunter. After that, we decided to put away all pictures of his mom, Deb.

Mom went with me to my dental appointment on October 27 to watch Hunter. Their waiting room had a small play area for children. I explained to Hunter that he could stay with Granny and play. "Hunter, here are the toys and books. They have a little barn too. You may play and wait with Granny. I must get my teeth cleaned and will be back soon." Hunter seemed OK with that idea.

Hunter was very loud while playing. Even so, that did not seem to bother anyone. I felt tense because I did not want him to disrupt or distress others. It was not long before Hunter began to become upset. He wanted to be with me. They allowed him to come into the examining room. He was fascinated with all the equipment! Hunter moved around and around the examining chair. This allowed Hunter to follow the hygienists' procedures better. Of course, he would not sit in a chair and watch! Oh no, he needed to see every instrument.

We made it through that exam. I was grateful for the kindness of the hygienist and staff. They still remember how tiny he was, how developmentally delayed, and how very curious. I am smiling now. They are still taking care of my dental procedures. They often remark how far he has come. Yes, he has!

I put Hunter and Mom in the car upon leaving the dentist's office. My telephone rang. It was Deb's new CPS worker, Kenneth. I informed Mom and Hunter that I needed to take the call. I then stepped outside of the car to continue the conversation. Kenneth asked questions about Deb. I did not hold back information. I told Kenneth about Deb's truancy in school, her mom, Monica, and stepfather's decision to put alarms on Deb's bedroom window, and how Deb, at age twelve, had escaped out her bedroom window to engage in sex with her twenty-one-year-old neighbor. When Deb was sixteen, Monica did not know how to manage Deb's behavior. Monica and I discussed the options that Monica thought might work. Nothing had yet changed Deb's expeditions or tendencies. Finally, Monica signed Deb up to attend a boot camp for troubled youth in Sexton Spring. I informed Kenneth that the boot camp kicked Deb out. She had been mingling with the other sex. That was a violation of their rules. I also told him of calls I received from Monica regarding Deb's activities after the police arrested Fred. Kenneth thanked me for the information.

CHAPTER 6

I had been watching for the relocation notice of our guardianship. The clerk in Deb's county had stated that they would "probably" switch the guardianship over to our county. That had not yet happened. I let Deb know that I had not received the notice of change to the guardianship. She replied, "That should have been done a long time ago."

I needed to research guardianship in general and specifically for our state. I began researching and studying Tennessee requirements regarding guardianships. I took it upon myself to file a petition to change the guardianship location to our county. Deb made comments, which led me to believe that she was getting ready to file a petition to terminate the guardianship.

She was in no position to do so. She was angry, in another relationship, and unstable emotionally. It was not a suitable environment for Hunter. Hunter had developed bonds with people within our circle. He had a solid medical team around him. The Early on childhood team was preparing to enroll Hunter in early childhood special education. The timing was not healthy for Hunter.

I then notified Deb that I intended to petition for the guardianship to be changed to our county. Deb stated that she was all right with that. I kept Deb informed of the status. The same judge who granted the original petition accepted the petition to change. The judge scheduled the hearing for November 19, 2015. Deb received a copy of the notice of the hearing and its schedule.

I remember the hearing day well. After we arrived, Brian, Hunter, and I waited outside the courtroom until it was time to go in. I paced up and down the corridor. Occasionally, I would glance out the window to see if I could see Deb. I was thinking and arguing with myself. I was questioning if I should call Deb to remind her. After complex and personal reflections, I decided not to call her. I still paced, hoping to see her arrive. I so wanted to call her. Yet I knew that her showing up or not would tell where her heart indeed was.

It came time to go into the courtroom. We sat in the back of the courtroom with Hunter. Hunter quietly played on the courtroom bench. We had brought a small toy car for him to play with. Those on the court's docket had to wait until called. That included us. Other cases came before ours. Occasionally, Hunter got a little restless. We would look at him, put a finger up to our lips, and quietly say, "Shh." He would immediately settle right down. He did not cause any disruption.

Finally, it was time for our case. The judge asked if Deb was there. We stated that she had not come. He quickly reviewed the paperwork. Seven days before the hearing, I had sent the judge the recommended cover letter with all the supporting documentation. So it did not take him long to review the petition. He quickly granted the petition. Next, the judge stated that we could now go to the clerk's office to obtain the final supporting paperwork. The clerk instructed us to take them to our county to complete relocating the guardianship.

As we turned to leave, I held Hunter; a group of lawyers were up front waiting to talk to the judge, but the judge addressed us. "Who is this little boy?"

I turned and replied, "Your Honor, this is Hunter." I then looked down at Hunter and said, "Hunter, do you want to tell the judge thank you?"

Hunter turned toward the judge, said, and signed, "Tank oo." Hunter could not pronounce his words correctly yet. Then Hunter said, "Lub oo." Hunter's comments brought a slight chuckle within the courtroom. His comments warmed my heart. The memory still warms my heart.

We left the courthouse after completing our stop in the clerk's office. We left to return home. It had been a long and emotional day. It was a four-hour trip one way for us. I was emotionally drained. My heart was disappointed that Deb did not show up.

That evening, at 9:54 p.m., I received a text message from Deb. I was in bed and almost asleep. Her message was, "Please tell me court was canceled and that I did not miss the chance to see my son. I just realized what the date is. I have been overwhelmed at work. I am sorry it is so late … but I need to know." I chose not to reply to her until the next day.

I replied via text at 7:04 a.m., "No, the court had not been canceled. I am sorry that you are so overwhelmed that you could not set a reminder on your phone." Then I further informed her that it took the judge less than three minutes to grant the petition. I knew that reply would not make Deb happy. She was not pleased with my remarks at all. She replied that she did not need a "sarcastic" reply. She further stated that I did not understand how hard she tried to get Hunter back.

It was becoming increasingly apparent that Deb was not and would never be in a healthy emotional state to raise Hunter. We knew that Deb was bipolar and had panic attacks, anxiety, and anger issues. Brian and I still did not feel that we wanted to adopt. Once again, we were still hoping that Deb would choose to change. To do that, she needed to stay with counseling. Yet I realized that adoption might become a real possibility.

I always tried to keep Monica and Deb informed about Hunter's health and developmental issues. Monica and I discussed the possibility of our adopting Hunter. This was not the first time we had discussed that we might have to adopt him. During this conversation, Monica voiced her concerns about our age. She worried Hunter would feel abandoned again if anything happened to us. I was open to Monica and Butch raising Hunter if something did happen to us. However, I was not comfortable with that.

We continued in that discussion. "Monica, don't you think that you will visit us, we will see you, you will call Hunter, and a bond will develop? Remember, we are intelligent and would make sure that happens. All of Hunter's medical help is here, he has friends, and he is getting needed therapy." Monica did not respond to those comments. I had a gut feeling that I knew why. If Monica had been honest, the truth was that she would have found a way to return Hunter to Deb. At what point or how I did not know.

On December 2, 2015, Deb called and asked if she could visit Hunter. She wanted to come either that weekend or the following one. She was having difficulties with her car and wanted to take care of them. Once again, Deb approached the subject of bringing someone with her. Once again, we said no.

She was able to come on December 5. I thought it would be fun for her and Hunter to decorate Christmas cookies. I had them all baked and ready for decorating. She arrived at about 2:25 p.m. I had put on soft Christmas music for relaxing background noise. This visit went well. Deb stayed off her FB and phone. She interacted with Hunter this time. He still did not call her mom. However, he did seem all right with her presence.

Hunter had come down with a little bit of a cold. Deb and I decided to stay home and not go to church the next day. Brian went to church while we stayed home. However, we did all go out to eat afterward. Once we came home, Deb left to go home. Hunter was comfortable with her leaving. Hunter had now accepted her presence and her departure. Hunter felt secure in our home and with us.

Deb did call and talk with Brian and Hunter for about two minutes on December 24, 2015. She wanted to wish Hunter and us a merry Christmas. She told Hunter that she loved him and missed him. I was out shopping, so I did not hear the tone of the conversation. Nor did I observe Hunter's body language.

CHAPTER 7

Early On sessions began to wind down. We were at the point where it was time to develop an IFP (individualized family plan). Heavens! I had no idea what that was. Both Brian and I had great jobs, raised our children, had our insurance, and now were learning and experiencing something entirely new. At times, it was overwhelming. The Early On team had informed us that at age three Hunter would have to attend an early-childhood special education class. The state required Hunter to participate in the district. I had to trust these women who represented the Early On developmental team for the area. They were great ladies. Still, I felt like I was in over my head. Things often felt outside of my control. We were in a guardianship position and limited in choice.

Hunter and I went to the Blue Mountain Elementary School and met Beverly, one of our Early On team members. Beverly, Hunter, and I visited the Blue Mountain Elementary School's early-childhood special education class. We observed the room's teacher and its students. I noticed young students who had behavioral challenges. Their behavioral challenges were more than Hunter's. However, Hunter still was not speaking well. I knew Hunter had to attend the special education class. I was a little too concerned about how the classroom atmosphere might impact him.

We later held an IEP (individualized education plan) meeting. That put things in motion for Hunter to begin school after he became three years old. Hunter would have additional resources specific to developmental delays. Hunter was eligible for a school speech therapist and occupational therapist.

Hunter was approaching his third birthday and the start of his early-childhood special education class. Deb had called on January 14 to inform me that she planned to spend Hunter's birthday with us. I was glad that she was thinking that way. I hoped she would become more involved with Hunter. She had started working in a home health care position. Deb stated that she had dropped one client and started a new job. I asked her what it was, and she told me that it was shoveling snow, snowplowing, and sprinkling salt for a company. Later, I learned that it was for the landscaping company that Maxton worked for.

Deb was not dealing well with caring for her home health care clients. She became emotionally involved. Often, she would state that she was "an emotional wreck." That was a phrase I became accustomed to hearing. It is now a day before Hunter's birthday. Deb called to say that she would not be coming. She had developed a cold. She stated that she would call him the next day on his birthday. Deb did call Hunter. There was nothing remarkable about that call. Hunter was happy with our birthday plans, and he was accustomed to being with us. I will note that Deb never sent Hunter any cards or gifts after we became his guardians.

Hunter started his Early On special education class. He began after his third birthday in January 2016. This was for the 2015–2016 school year. The team observed his behaviors and developed a visual chart for him. I still laugh at that chart. Hunter did not understand the visual chart. Hunter was developmentally delayed. His delay contributed to his initial response to the visual chart. He had other issues. He had only had his hearing aid for about four months, was an only child, and did not know how to react.

At first, I stayed within the classroom and functioned as an interpreter. I also helped get the children from one activity to the next. At lunchtime, staff would place the visual chart in front of Hunter. He was to point to what he wanted, and they would point at what the next item was for him and his class to do. He often got angry and would throw the visual away. His reactions were usually when he did not want to do the required activity. Eventually, I was able to be outside of the classroom. However, I stayed within the school building, readily available when needed. The staff allowed me to come in when the children had free time or lunch. Hunter did not adjust well. For the first two to three weeks, he had nightmares. In the classroom, he often burst out in anger.

This was concerning to me. At birth, Hunter received the diagnosis of hypoxic ischemic encephalopathy and had seizures. My mind wondered if there might be something more causing these outbursts. I consulted with Dr. Kelly and shared my concern. Dr. Kelly agreed. Dr. Kelly felt that we should have Hunter seen by a neurologist and have the neurologist do a complete workup. I informed Deb of this appointment. I made a point of telling Deb of Hunter's changes in health or significant appointments. It still was my heart's desire that she would get things together. Despite her instability and lack of consistent interest in Hunter, I still prayed that she would be able to one day parent Hunter.

In the Sam's Club bathroom, my mom fell on Sunday, February 22, 2016. We had gone to Sam's after church. I stayed in the pharmacy aisle while she went to the handicap area to use the restroom. After about two minutes, a lady came and flagged me down. She asked, "Are you Mary?"

I replied, "Yes, I am."

She said, "Your mom has fallen in the bathroom. We have called an ambulance." Somehow, my mother had lost her balance. She fell backward and hit her head in the front corner of the stall.

She must have also twisted her leg. I texted Brian and told him to take Hunter home. I had to ride in the ambulance with my mother. Mom had been severely injured. She was in intense pain. We learned she had broken her right hip. The hospital staff went to work to get her into the Brookside rehab center as soon as Mom would be strong enough to go there. On February 26, 2016, they put her in a wheelchair and rolled her over to the Brookside.

The hospital and the Brookside were only about two blocks apart. The bumpy ride was not easy on Mom. She was not able to stand on her own. The staff had to lift her with a hoist. Then they managed to move her by using either a wheelchair or sometimes, with assistance, a walker. It took weeks of therapy to regain her strength to walk with a walker.

I now took Hunter to and from school. In addition, I visited Mom and attended her therapy sessions. The responsibilities began to have a substantial emotional toll on me. I was still in the process of getting Hunter into seeing a neurologist. I remember simply breaking out into tears as I dropped Hunter off at his class one day. I sat near his classroom, fighting to remain calm and collected. It was an exhausting day.

Hunter's teacher and staff knew the amount of responsibility on my schedule. This day, they gave me the business card of Donna Fry. Donna Fry was affiliated with a support group for those who were caring for their kin's children. She had firsthand experience. I would later meet with her. Donna became a major source of support and information. She cheered me on and up. We would meet and share our heartaches.

We finally received a referral to a neurologist at the Tennessee Children's Hospital in Grand View, Tennessee. Dr. Sam Dodge would see us on April 1, 2016. Deb wanted to see Hunter. We arranged for Deb, Marten, Sophia, Annie, Alden, and Hunter's step-grandmother to meet us at a play area in a mall after his procedure.

The neurologist scheduled a one-hour EEG appointment. I sat on the hospital bed with Hunter on my lap. They then hooked him up with the wires and put on the movie *Cars*. He got a little restless. However, they did catch a quick spike or two that might have represented evidence of seizure activity. It was not enough yet. They wanted to follow up with another visit and scheduled a twenty-four-hour EEG.

After the appointment, we went to the mall. We saw Deb approaching us. I asked Hunter if he wanted to say hi to his mom. Hunter quickly grabbed my hand and said, "No!" Marten and Sophia stood by and observed.

Deb and her step-grandmother sat next to each other. Brian and I sat next to Deb and her step-grandmother. Deb spent time on her phone. Occasionally, she would take pictures and speak briefly to Annie and Alden. Deb spent most of her time talking with her step-grandmother. It was an awkward atmosphere.

There was a moment when Deb had her phone out, looking at pictures or messages, and Hunter approached her. He stood by her, curious about the phone. It was an ideal moment for her to talk with and play with him. However, she did not. She was sad and had tears because Hunter initially did not want to say hi to her. She could have tried to bond with Hunter. Deb missed an excellent opportunity.

Hunter was still having a rough time adapting to school and the classroom. There were about three children who were very high-strung. Hunter's classroom was laid out as follows: The students' cubbies were within steps upon entering. The bathrooms were located on the right side of the entry wall and the other on the far-left-side entry wall. Upon entering, one could see the round table. It served as a learning area and their lunch table. On the wall, to the left of the round table, was a long kitchen counter. It contained a sink and cabinets above and below the counter. The cabinets stored supplies. On the backside of the cubbies were shelves containing supplies and books. Looking past the round lunch table, you could see a craft table. The craft table could seat ten chairs on each side. This table was for crafts and free time with Duplo or other Legos.

Also, upon entering the classroom, the windows were located on the back wall. Old-fashioned heat registers heated the room just under the window ledge. A projector screen and the teacher's work area were to the right of the windows. The staff had attempted to block off the teacher's work area by adding storage cubicles. The work area contained the teacher's computer system. The staff used the computer to show educational videos or YouTube songs. In front of the projector screen was the student's circle rug. The circle rug had each student's name tag placed where the student was to sit or stand. They used this area to listen to stories, watch or participate in YouTube videos, or learn new concepts.

One day, I came into the classroom. It was free time after lunch. Two aides were talking with each other in the lunch area. They were not paying attention to the activities surrounding them. The following events were happening within the room: Children played with Duplos around the craft table. The little Down Syndrome boy, who walked with a walker, was heading to the teacher's work area. The teacher was trying to head him off from reaching her computer area.

A little girl was walking near the teacher. The teacher continued to proceed toward the Down Syndrome boy, attempting to redirect him away from the computer area. Suddenly, the little girl again passed within the teacher's eyesight. The teacher noticed that the little girl's pants were on backward. The teacher reached the little Down Syndrome boy and was gently redirecting him out of the teacher's work area. She was also asking the girl to go to the restroom. "Maddie, your pants are on backward. Please go to the restroom. I will come there soon and help you to put your pants on correctly." After the teacher made her request, Maddie went toward the bathroom. Maddie was also starting to pull her pants down, and her little buttocks were beginning to be visible. Yet the aides were still not assisting the teacher.

In the meantime, chaos was breaking out at the Duplo table. I will simply call this boy "Mean Boy." Mean Boy was walking down the length of the table, taking children's Duplo projects away from them. The first boy was Hunter. Hunter simply gave Mean Boy his Duplo. The next boy began to wrestle with Mean Boy. The aides were still merely talking and ignoring the ongoing activities. The teacher was still redirecting the Down Syndrome boy. So I went behind the two struggling boys and began to put my arms around their shoulders gently. Soon I heard the teacher loudly exclaim, "Mary!" I was following proper protocol. However, there must have been a potential liability issue. So I backed off.

Mean Boy continued to the next boy and took his Duplo. That young, kind, redheaded boy turned to me and said, "See? I gave him mine."

I replied, "That was kind of you." Then Mean Boy went to the last boy. That boy would have nothing to do with Mean Boy taking his Duplo, which was now a rather large construction. Still, it did fit into Mean Boy's hand. They fought, and then Mean Boy swung that Duplo project forcefully into that boy's cheek!

The Down Syndrome boy was now safely outside the teacher's work area. The teacher instructed Mean Boy to sit down while checking on the last boy's face. Mean Boy got up and began to walk around the room. Finally, one aide went to try to encourage Mean Boy to sit down.

I was amazed that the aide did extraordinarily little to help. Fortunately, the classroom was next to the principal's office. The principal eventually came in and took control of the class situation. This was *not* a safe environment for Hunter or other children.

Hunter's speech therapist had informed me that Hunter had the strength of modeling behaviors. Since Hunter had been in our care, we had made a point of exposing Hunter to positive behaviors. This was not all right with me. I pulled Hunter from the class. Of course, now the school was dealing with an impact on their finances. They wanted me to reconsider. My response was, "Until you can prove to me that you have resolved the safety issue, Hunter will not be returning."

Two weeks later, the principal asked me to come in to discuss their resolution. She and the teacher reassured me that they would immediately remove the children from the classroom if Mean Boy again misbehaved. I made an appointment to discuss it further with Hunter present. They explained their strategies. Hunter was extremely uncomfortable being around the principal. However, I decided to let him back in the classroom. I chose to continue to stay close by. I sat on a bench outside his classroom. Periodically, I would peer into the classroom window. I had done the right thing! The result: Mean Boy became an advocate and a helper of both Hunter and the Down Syndrome boy.

CHAPTER 8

In June 2016, Hunter's contentment continued to grow. He was beginning to cooperate more in speech therapy. He loved my mom, known to all as "Granny," and played with the next-door neighbor children. We had a garden. He loved to be outside. Hunter's first experience with his bike helmet generated a scream from Hunter. He had a sensory processing disorder too. I could not resist taking a picture of him screaming the first time he had the helmet on. It was a short-lived scream. Eventually, Hunter became accustomed to wearing the helmet. However, the picture is a little hilarious. Do not get me wrong. I balanced compassion with humor. We dealt with Hunter's emotional and sensory needs with compassion and patience. I will admit it. I may have silently chuckled just a bit when Hunter screamed.

We made sure that Hunter had places to play in our large yard: a sandbox, a swing, and a teeter-totter. He had fun exploring our woods. I remember going into the garden one day to weed. Hunter wanted to help. He was now a little over three and a half years old. I proceeded to try teaching him what weeds looked like. Our beets were merely coming up. Oh well! You guessed it! He pulled one row of my beets! Another weeding lesson would be necessary. He felt so proud of his accomplishment though.

Mom, a.k.a. "Granny," loved Hunter. Those two were developing a great bond. He could con her into giving him a ride on her walker seat. It accomplished two things: it gave Mom much-needed exercise and gave Hunter a fun time. He often had the biggest smile on his face and would call out, "Beep, beep!" They still have a special relationship.

June was also the month when Deb's calls portrayed more evidence of her unstable emotional insecurities. She already had gone through so many jobs: Deb's first job was with ICab the previous year. ICab fired Deb after five months.

After ICab, Deb took a position with a home health care company. Deb then quit that job and accepted another home health care company position. I am not sure if she left that job or if she was fired. Finally, Deb called to say she had gotten a new job working for a telecommunications company. She was not sure what position she would have with them. When I asked her, she stated that it would be in their warranty department. I do not think that job ever panned out.

Deb had been angry during those times. I do not know for sure, but it was sometime during her career with ICab or the home health care. I know that she told me that she had gotten incredibly angry with someone. She stated that she wanted to "Punch them!" Instead, she said that she had punched the wall. She had hit hard enough that she had broken her wrist. She had to have a cast. Deb hated the discomfort of the form. Then she said, "I was so mad and tired of it. I just ripped it off!"

I became more convinced that we would end up adopting Hunter. How to delicately go about it, to retain a good relationship, was something I prayed about. I wanted to be diligent and obtain strong advice. Fortunately, we had a good Christian friend who specialized in adoption. I asked her if she could be my Moses. Might we meet and discuss the issues? She was my rock and strength. She met me, at no charge, after hours. Maxine specialized in adoption. The initial visit was so I could inform Maxine of the events thus far.

Doing so helped Maxine to determine if I was thinking clearly and correctly. It was necessary to keep Hunter's best interests first. She agreed with me—we should adopt. Yes, she asked about his grandmother, Monica. Would she or could she adopt? I explained that the option would not be in Hunter's best interest.

I provided Maxine with my reasoning: Monica lived in the mountains of Montana and was teaching. Monica's husband did not want to work but was. Their son, Jackson, had made poor decisions: fathered children and lost custody of them. Monica and Butch would visit with Jackson's daughter and sneak him for a visit. In addition, there were indications that they would try to return Hunter to Deb should they adopt him. I took to heart her advice and continued to pray. I did want Deb to be a part of the decision. At the very least, I wanted her to willingly consent.

Hunter, Brian, and I went to the beach and played with the neighbors. We enrolled Hunter in gymnastic sessions. Then in June, we took a long trip to visit our daughters and their families. After these visits, I became fully convinced that God wanted us to adopt Hunter.

Brian and I did take Hunter to visit Monica and Butch as we stated we would. We did this even though we became convinced that we would adopt. We wanted Hunter to bond with his grandmother, Monica.

They had moved to Montana. They had always wanted to retire "in the mountains of Montana." Monica had accepted a teaching position there. Butch did not want to work anymore. He had mentioned that he was willing to be a "stay-at-home-mom" for Hunter if he were ever to come there. Monica had no idea if or when we might adopt Hunter. I think she might have felt that it would not come to that.

We headed on our vacation. We planned to first visit Monica and Butch for a day or two. Then we would head to Ohio to see

Belinda and Devan. We drove eight or nine hours, made any necessary pit stops, and stopped at hotels or motels if tired.

Monica and Butch lived in the mountains. The mountains were steep. They were far from any large town or city. She taught in an older brick school building. It housed preschool to senior high schoolers. The total number of students in attendance was around 250. The students, who lived in the mountains, rode the bus to school.

They had purchased a tiny, older home. It needed repairs. Butch had been a building contractor. He had remodeled their new home before our visit. As I said, it was *small*. It was about the size of our great room. We could feel the floors moving as we walked on them. Butch had done an excellent job at making it look aesthetically pleasing. Yet it certainly was not sturdy.

It was mid to late afternoon when we had arrived. Monica showed me a large watermelon she had purchased and a gallon of chocolate milk. Before we came, she had asked me what Hunter would eat. I had informed her that he would eat watermelon and drink chocolate milk. I did not want her to go out of her way to purchase food for Hunter. He was extremely fussy about what he would eat. They did have a small, fenced-in backyard. Monica informed me that they had lots of ticks. She also stated that they had not cleaned up their dogs' messes. So, if we wanted to take Hunter out there, she recommended that we "watch where we step."

Hunter was now three and a half years old. He still loved to ride in a car and traveled exceptionally well. We took PediaSure for him and packed other foods. He would eat cheese sticks, raisins, and organic fruit gummies. He would also eat pancakes and waffles. Hunter still ate in patterns. We still could not cut pancakes, toast, and waffles. They had to be perfect in shape and size, and now nothing could be added to them.

I forgot to explain to Monica what kind of watermelon and chocolate milk we bought. That became an issue of contention and sorrow later. I should have said that Hunter would only eat seedless watermelon, that we cut it into small, uniform pieces, and that the chocolate milk was whole and organic. I would equally mix his chocolate milk with organic white milk.

We had brought enough PediaSure that I knew Hunter would not need to drink any chocolate milk that they had. However, Monica kept reminding me that she had it. I felt that it would be rude not to give Hunter the chocolate milk. So I would give it to him but not often and not much. Thank goodness, they never offered the watermelon. I did not have to deal with any explanations about that.

I want to back up now and address how we felt when we arrived. Remember, Hunter had traveled for two days, it was his first long trip, he had already lived with us for over one and a half years, and he was tired. They had a dog, and Hunter liked their dog. Their dog was large. At times, their dog did cause Hunter to be a bit apprehensive. Monica and Butch's greetings felt strained to us. I felt unwelcomed. It was simply an uncomfortable and awkward atmosphere.

Hunter began to stand and spin in circles. He had not yet received the diagnosis of autism. I did not know that what he had been doing both that day and previously was echolalia. Nor did I know that his spinning was called stimming. Stimming is a method used to self-regulate. Echolalia is the act of repeating phrases said rather than responding to what people say or ask. We could make a statement or ask a question of Hunter, and he would repeat what we had said. That is echolalia. It was not until about one and a half years later that I learned about stimming and echolalia. At this point, Hunter only had the right hearing aid. He also was not enunciating words or sounds correctly—especially those in the high-frequency range.

Monica had put a television show on for Hunter and held him on her lap. I have a beautiful picture of the two of them together.

Monica accidentally dropped something, quickly grabbed it up, and expressively said, "Way to go!" Hunter laughed at that.

Monica began to make a game of it. Soon Hunter was saying, "Way to go!" He was having an enjoyable time. It was nice to see. I explained to Monica that Hunter often repeated phrases and spun. Her reply was, "Maybe it is just because he's three." Her tone implied that it had nothing to do with his diagnosis of "hearing impaired" or "developmentally delayed." She was very aware of those diagnoses.

Monica and Butch stated that they planned to take us out for breakfast and dinner the next day. They also wanted to take us to visit a special lookout. Oh my goodness! I am shaking my head as I remember that next day! There were good times, fun times, and uncomfortable times. *Focus, Mary. Talk about bedtime and the following day.*

Brian and Butch were visiting together. Hunter was tired, so I got him ready for bed. They had started a movie or show on what was to be our bedroom's television. They did it for Hunter, who was restless and having difficulty getting to sleep.

He wanted Papa too. I went out to the living room and asked if Brian could come into bed shortly. I explained that Hunter was restless and wanted Brian. I hope you will see how their later shared reactions become a part of my heartache. Brian did come to bed, and we all slept well.

The following day, as I was changing and dressing Hunter, he said his very first sentence: "Go home. Go home." His voice was so sad. I told him that we would be doing fun things today and head home the next day.

First, we went to a favorite little restaurant of Butch's. He was so proud of the size of their pancakes. I knew that Hunter would eat a small pancake. I ordered a small pancake for him and milk. I ordered bacon with my pancake.

Hunter's pancake came. His pancake was giant and not perfectly round. I knew that Hunter would not eat it. I asked the server if they could make a smaller pancake for Hunter. She would have asked the chef to do so. However, Butch loudly exclaimed with pride, "That is their smallest pancake!" I did not repeat my request. Hunter did not eat any of his pancakes. He did, however, do a first. He tried and ate a piece of my bacon. I was so glad that he did and that we had PediaSure.

From there, we went to the special lookout. It was a large building that overlooked a dam. Hunter loved to explore and run. That was precisely what he did. He ran and ran. He would stop and try to look out of the binoculars. Then he would immediately take off running again.

Occasionally, he would stop and continue to spin. I was in hot pursuit of him—all the time! Butch did not like Hunter's antics. Butch especially did not like Hunter's spinning. Oh well; that was who Hunter was. I was ready to intervene if needed. I only had to redirect once or twice because of other visitors' presence.

After we left, we stopped for ice cream. Next, we returned to their house for a quick break. They had told us of a five-acre parcel of land they had purchased. It was about a mile away from their current home. They were in the process of clearing and getting ready to build a small cabin. They had planned to retire to their little house. Butch had been cutting down trees and wanted to let Hunter watch him cut down a tree.

We went to see their land and watched him cut a tree down. Monica informed us that there was poison ivy there. They had killed "most of it." Brian was allergic to poison ivy. We did not know if Hunter was allergic. Remember, we also knew they had ticks. I would not let Hunter down. I held him the whole time.

That did not sit well with either Monica or Butch. There was no way that I would cave in and put Hunter down. It was now getting close to dinnertime. They took us to this charming and quaint restaurant. The only thing on the menu that I knew Hunter would eat was ice cream. That was what I ordered for him. The food was delicious, and we enjoyed the restaurant. However, I did not appreciate Butch's disdain at the food we had requested for Hunter.

I knew that I could give Hunter foods we had with us later. Butch and Hunter finished eating before Monica, Brian, and I. Hunter was getting restless. Butch asked if he could take Hunter for a walk around the block. I said sure.

We returned to their home and relaxed a little. Hunter sat on Butch's lap for a while. Monica showed me a little area they had converted for her office. It was nice. Later, we readied ourselves for bed and our departure the following day.

The following day, we said our goodbyes and headed for Ohio. Once again, Hunter traveled well. He had playful fun with Belinda and Devan. They had a big yard and small dogs. They understood Hunter and his eccentric behaviors. It was a comfortable atmosphere.

The next day, we went to the Children's Museum in Ohio. Hunter loved it there. He ran full speed from one thing to the next. I had a challenging time keeping up with him. His favorite floor was where the cars were. They had an area where he could take apart tires. There were places for children to play in the sand, water, and with instruments. There was an area of dinosaurs and train displays. So much more! It was great fun.

I had fun taking pictures of our visits and adventures while with Monica, Butch, Belinda, and Devan. Pictures of places we went and the people we visited. I was a new user of my phone. I had not been on FB long. While at Belinda's, I discovered that I could share pictures. The first pictures I saw were recent while visiting Belinda and Devan. Those were the ones I shared first on FB. Then I posted pictures about our visit with Monica and Butch. Monica reacted in anger on FB. Her comment was, "They visited us first!"

Deb called us the next day after the visits with our daughters. Hunter and I had been outside playing. Deb had contacted us on our landline, and Brian picked up the call. She wanted to talk to

Hunter and me. Brian let Deb know that he would go outside and let me know. After Brian informed me, I called her back on my cell phone.

Hunter and I were sitting on a bit of bench in front of our flower garden. I sensed that Monica had encouraged Deb to call us, especially since it was only one day after returning from our vacation with Hunter. Hunter still was not talking much or enunciating words well. I put the phone on speaker and translated Hunter's responses to Deb. He did respond with a "lub oo" to Deb. This was after she told him that she loved him.

It was a beautiful, sunny day. Hunter liked nothing more than to run and play outside. His attention to the call was short-lived. I then took the phone off speaker and chatted with Deb. It was a strange call—not entirely unfamiliar, but her tone felt forced. It was as if she thought she should talk about something or anything. Our phone connection was often interrupted. I would call her back. I was not sure why we kept losing connection.

Her conversation again centered around her emotional state. Deb stated that one of her clients had passed away. This made her sad. Understandably so. However, she simply kept repeating how hard it was and how she did not think that she could work in that profession any longer. Of course, I sympathized with her. Yet I knew how Deb could overreact and bend truths. I was not sure that the call had anything to do with sharing her sadness. Instead, it was more likely a result of Monica encouraging her to make the call. Deb had stopped calling or contacting us regularly. The timing of Deb's call was incredibly coincidental.

About four or five days later, we received a FB message from Belinda. She had copied and sent a message that Butch had sent to Brian's sister Tootsie. Butch had told Tootsie that it was no wonder Hunter was spinning all the time because all "she did was to feed him sugar!" Further, she had "demanded Brian go to bed." Tootsie had shared Butch's message and reached out to Belinda. Tootsie asked Belinda what she knew or felt about that.

Belinda stated that she trusted her mom and dad. She said that they were doing an excellent job with Hunter.

So Tootsie replied to Butch, stating that he should have addressed his concerns to her brother. She further noted that her brother was healthy and happy; she supported him. Brian was upset regarding the comments Butch had made. Brian stated, "That is not true. You did not demand I go to bed. We are a team, and we work together." We did not directly address either Butch or Monica about their communications with Tootsie.

Butch then posted on FB: "I didn't know that a visit to our home was to approve it." The negative posts by Monica, Butch, and Deb made me choose to block them. They remained blocked for a long time. I still have Butch and Deb blocked. Both continue to have characters that I do not fully trust.

Our oldest daughter, Monica, used to call me often. She used to be a rock of support for me. We would share how we felt about certain television shows. Our favorite shows were *America's Got Talent* and *The Voice*. Then, too, she would call and share concerns she was going through with her daughter, Deb, or her son, Jackson. In a way, I was also a rock for Monica. Both of her children had very troubled childhoods. Both Monica and her children had made terrible choices in life.

Now, Monica was no longer a rock of support. My heart was beginning to break. Yet I continued to protect and nurture Hunter. That did not mean that I was not sad about losing our relationship with our oldest daughter. I hope you understand this journey is complex and not without loss. The heartaches we had gone through up to this point had been beyond difficult.

CHAPTER 9

July 2016 was busy with weekly speech therapies for Hunter. There were medical appointments for Mom.

Hunter's speech therapy, outside of school, was with a great therapist. In the first year of therapy, she would use incentives to minimize Hunter's sliding in and out of the chairs. The incentives were his favorite toys: cars, trucks, and fire trucks. At times, Hunter would become impatient with trying to say words and become frustrated. At those times, he would begin to yell the items he wanted: "Car!" "Truck!" ("Tuck!") He was still not enunciating well.

Hunter's speech therapist was now able, in his second year of therapy, to increase his attention by introducing games or toys like a barn set. This allowed her and me to point at an added item, say its name, and then ask Hunter to repeat the word.

Recently, I watched a video of me trying to get Hunter to speak in 2015. He had been getting in and out of a chair and then would take off running. As I was following him, I asked, "Hunter, what does a cow say?" Hunter gave no response. He simply scooted out of the chair. "Hunter, what does a duck say?" Again, no response. As I watched the video, I was surprised how calm my voice was and how I persevered. I continued and eventually received a response from Hunter. I asked Hunter, "What does a cow say?" He simply shook his head no. He was advancing in his ability to enunciate. Yet he had much more to achieve.

Then was our next weekend McClellan get-together at our home. This time Hunter was able to have fun. Monica decided not to join this time. She was in the process of getting her school curriculum ready for her class in the new school. Then, too, she had seen us in June.

Monica had sent me a private message after I mailed out the reminder of our annual get-together. Her words were angry. She stated that she felt no one in "her family" would make her feel welcomed. I was sure that we would have. I was also sure that her presence might have made family members feel a bit awkward. I do know that we would have avoided discussing the events and conversations that followed our visit to their home.

On August 10, 2016, I wrote a letter to Deb. I mailed Deb's copy to her through a return receipt process. I chose that method for legal reasons. The first paragraph went as follows:

> You know that we are very much aware that the decision you made, for the sake of your son, had to be a tough one to make. Yes, the system. and the courts put you into the position to choose between your family having guardianship over him versus having Hunter taken away from you. Yet, that does not minimize the difficult and courageous decision you made.

The letter then went on to list all that Hunter had accomplished or experienced under our care. It also included how we had addressed his behavior problems, our involvement with the system, our ability to obtain SSI Disability for him, and how we could further help Hunter going forward.

We asked her to pray about it and not choose to be angry—to consider, pray, and let us know her answer. In the letter, I also stated the following:

> Know this, you are his mom and will always be referred to him as his mom. We are his great grandparents—who he calls Papa and Mama. Should he question why you willingly terminated your parental rights, we will tell him that you loved him enough to allow him to be raised by your grandparents. Your grandparents who love you and him. We will also explain that you understood that we could better provide for him now and in the future.

It, of course, was a much longer letter. It was a difficult letter. Yet I did it in love.

Deb called me two weeks after she received it. Deb explained that she had been camping with Maxton and his family. Deb shared that his family camped together once every year. There was not any anger in her voice. We discussed the things pointed out in the letter. I told her to take her time and reminded her to pray about it again.

I continued in prayer and examined my mind and heart. I began to study adoption—specifically, the laws in our state regarding adoption and the processes involved. I knew two legal things would be coming up shortly: first, filing of the guardianship annual review was due one year after its implemented date, and second, petitioning for adoption. However, Brian and I knew that we had to protect Hunter whether we successfully adopted him or not.

We made an appointment with our lawyer. Immediately, we started the process of drawing up wills, medical power of attorneys, and a McClellan family trust. We had the lawyers include statements to protect and provide for Hunter. I began meeting with my attorney to discuss the adoption process. Our trip to Monica and Butch's and their following remarks made it apparent that Hunter would need protection.

Even though I knew we would adopt Hunter, I wanted Deb included in that process. That is why I sent her the registered return receipt letter in August 2016.

We still had Hunter in speech therapy in August 2016. In addition, we began counseling sessions with Community Mental Health for Hunter. He sure was a busy little boy: speech therapy, CMH sessions, trips to take Mom to the doctors, his appointments at the hearing clinic, and beginning gymnastics.

On August 27, 2016, we met dear friends nearby. They met Hunter for the first time. They were so glad that we had stepped up to be there for Hunter. A marina was nearby. We took a walk to the marina area. Hunter loved walking the planks within the boat docks. Hunter thought the yachts were great. He laughed and ran with pure joy. What a fun day!

September 3, 2016, was one day before our wedding anniversary. It was a lovely day outside. Brian, Hunter, and I headed to the beach. Happy people filled the beach. People were simply enjoying the day before school began. We had a lovely surprise while there. A middle-aged gentleman was putting on a show of giant bubbles! We all gathered and watched in amazement. Children were trying to catch the bubbles. Hunter stood right next to Brian. He could not restrain his excitement. Eventually, Hunter became brave enough to join the other children. They were all trying to catch the bubbles. Hunter did not join in trying to catch the bubbles immediately. Both the bubbles and the number of children made him a little anxious. I was standing near Hunter. Eventually, he got over the anxiety and joined in

Deb's county had granted the change on November 19, 2015. However, our county did not complete the process until January 7, 2016. I had to file the annual review of guardianship; its due date was by January 7, 2017. Even though I had questioned if we should adopt Hunter, I now knew that we would begin the process to adopt. We were willing to adopt whether Deb agreed or not. We knew it was what was best for Hunter. Yes, we had considered our ages. Yes, it was a bit scary. Yet, we still knew that was God's intent. We needed to trust in God's direction. But yikes!

In October, Deb called to talk. I did not know it then, but she was pregnant when she called. We had just gotten out of our church service. It was a Sunday morning. We had not even left the parking lot when my phone rang. It was Deb wanting to talk. First, she asked if it was a good time to talk. I responded, "Well, we just got out of the church. We are heading to Burger King like we usually do. But, yes, it is all right. We will be driving. There are hills. I can call you back if we lose connection. If you are OK with that, we can talk." Deb replied that she was.

She shared that she and Maxton had spent time helping his parents reroof their house. Deb stated that she had wanted to go up on the roof to help, but Maxton did not want her to do that. Those remarks should have given me a clue to ask why not, but I did not ask. We were now pulling into the Burger King parking lot. I informed her that we had arrived. Deb offered to call later. I sensed that she wanted to talk more. "Deb, I will let them go in, and we can talk more."

Then I said, "Brian, you all go in to eat. I can eat later. I will just talk with Deb more." He, Hunter, and Mom went into Burger King. I continued with Deb. "Deb, it is OK to talk. Is there something else you wanted to talk about?"

She said, "Grandma, I wanted you to know that I have not forgotten about your letter. I have been praying about you and Grandpa adopting Hunter."

I replied, "Deb, I am glad that you have been. It is good that you called. I have made an appointment with my lawyer. The appointment is to begin the process of adopting Hunter."

Deb's response was "What? I thought you could not adopt without a parent's permission!"

"Deb," I replied, "yes, you can. But it can get messy. Deb, we do not want messy. We want you involved. We want you to be a part of the process. I would like you to attend and stay involved."

Deb replied, "I don't think that I want to be there."

I said, "Deb, does that mean that you will not fight this?"

Deb replied, "No, I will not. But do I have to be there? What do I have to do?"

I answered, "Deb, I know that you must go in front of a judge and have your parental rights terminated. I can ask if that must happen here or if you may do it where you are. Would you like me to ask my lawyer?" Deb stated that she wanted me to do so. Much later, I learned that Deb had another baby boy in March 2017. Now knowing that, I imagine that, although she was angry, she accepted the fact that we were proceeding with adoption. She understood that she would not have won if she fought it. Deb also knew that she might risk losing custody of the child she was carrying.

I met with Maxine the following week. I had already researched how to petition the court to adopt. I obtained the appropriate forms and completed them for my appointment. My lawyer, Maxine, reviewed what I had provided her. She had only one slight change she wanted to make. She stated that it was just that, "slight," and would get back to me when it was complete. I informed her of my conversation with Deb. I asked if Deb had to present in front of the judge here or not. She stated that Deb could do it in her area. However, we would have to receive documentation showing that a judge had terminated Deb's parental rights. Next, I called and informed Deb that a judge in her area could terminate her parental rights. We then had to receive notification of the termination of her parental rights.

Deb was relieved that she could face a judge in her area to terminate her parental rights. Kudos to Deb. She did follow through and began the process. The termination of Deb's parental rights happened on December 28, 2016. I imagine that she must have appeared to be pregnant at that hearing. It was not until the following summer that I learned of her pregnancy.

However, I did not receive timely notification of the termination of Deb's parental rights. It was time for me to generate the annual review of our guardianship legally. Had I received timely notification of the termination of her parental rights, I would not have sent her a copy of the annual guardianship review. The laws legally required me to provide Deb with her copy of the annual review. I complied. How I wish I had known earlier of the termination. I could have ignored my legal obligation to provide her with a copy of the annual review.

I did so because I am ethical. I included the spreadsheet that laid out every medical visit, extracurricular activity, communication and visits with Deb, and all notations regarding each. Deb was furious when she received her copy. She stated, "You could have left out all those extra comments!"

I responded, "There were not enough lines on the form to include what they required of me. I called the clerk and asked if it would be acceptable to attach a spreadsheet. They told me that it was all right."

Deb, still livid, replied, "You lied! I saw him more than two times!"

I simply replied, "Deb, in the time frame that I had to report, you did not." She thought her visit on December 2, 2015, should have been included. It could not because our county did not complete the change of guardianship in 2015. That call did not go well.

Deb's call in October and her angry response to the annual review of guardianship occurred while Hunter was in his second year of early-childhood special education.

CHAPTER 10

In 2016–2017, Hunter was again in the early-childhood special education class at Blue Mountain Elementary. The open house was the Friday before school was to begin. They informed us that they had no teacher! The previous year's teacher had taken another position within the school system. In addition, another teacher, also within the school system, had accepted the position and backed out that Friday. They now had no teacher, had an aide, and were rushing to locate a substitute. Based on the previous year's experiences, I simply stated, "Unless you tell me that I cannot, I intend to be in that classroom to help." They did not deny me.

I began to stay in the classroom and help. This year, they gained an additional student who was autistic and fascinated with clocks and gears! He could be a challenge. He and I got along very well. I could get him to comply with anything. One day, the staff had given him a toy clock to hold. It was then time to leave for the day. He was *not* going to give up that clock! No number of reassurances by any staff member would get him to give it up, even when they stated that they would put it away for him and he could have it the next day. Finally, I gently took his hand, telling him that we could put the clock "right here," and he would be able to have it tomorrow. He responded by placing the clock down and left quietly.

One day, the substitute teacher went on a rampage—in front of the children, no less! She stated, "Why am I even here? I do not know what I am doing!" On and on she went.

I quietly stood by one of the aides and said, "Ann, I am so sorry that you are experiencing this. This is unacceptable! No staff member should behave this way in front of the students."

Eventually, they did find a teacher. She was a great teacher. I continued in the classroom for about two more months. Then they felt that my presence might be hindering Hunter. It did not show to be a fact. However, I continued to stay close by and available.

One day when I came to pick up Hunter, the autistic boy was the last to leave. The aide had already left the room. Only Hunter and I were immediately available. Suddenly, the autistic boy lunged toward the teacher, who was sitting in a chair, and grabbed her throat. He immediately began to choke her. He was powerful! She could not get him off, and she choked out, "Help me!" The aide immediately entered the room. Both the aide and I were able to release the autistic boy's grasp. It was not long after that that we no longer saw him in the classroom. Oh, how I loved that little boy. Understanding and gentle guidance were what he needed.

Hunter had episodes where he would become frustrated with their visual aids and angry again. Hunter would toss the visual when he was angry. Other times, he simply would scream and shove them out of the way. Honestly, the staff simply did not understand his degree of developmental delay. CMH tried to help.

I called for an IEP meeting; I was not witnessing or seeing results of positive change or growth in Hunter. I invited CMH to the meeting. At one point, Hunter got up, went to the circle rug, and tore off a student's taped down name. I knew why he did it. His speech teacher asked Hunter, "Hunter, why did you do that?"

Of course, Hunter did not answer. He could not answer. I knew why but said nothing as the meeting simply continued.

I felt like the meeting was not accomplishing anything. Even though the meeting was now about a one half hour over, I asked if I might read a couple of the last paragraphs from Jane Healy's book, *Different Learners*. Despite the team's silent objections, they allowed me to do so.

The sections talked about a young niece who was visiting her aunt. Her aunt asked her niece if she liked broccoli. To which she replied, "Why, yes I do." Dinner was finished. The aunt noticed that her niece had not eaten her broccoli. The aunt said, "I thought you liked broccoli." The niece replied, "Well, yes, I do. Just not enough to eat it." I then looked at the team and said, "I do not know if you care enough to teach however differently to be effective. But I do!" There was dead silence in the room. I then stated, "You want to know why Hunter tore the name label off? It was because it was no longer perfect. He simply wanted to fix it." Staff dismissed the meeting. The teacher went to a corner of the room in tears.

Hunter was also having ABA therapies during this second year of early-childhood special education. Mr. B. would come to our home to work with Hunter. There are two incidents I want to share. The first: Mr. B. had taken several geometric shapes out and placed them on the table. He had various sizes of circles, triangles, squares, and rectangles. Mr. B. then held up a triangle and asked, "Hunter, what shape goes with this?"

Hunter quickly reached over and picked up a circle. Then he removed the triangle from Mr. B.'s hands, held the triangle upside down, and placed the circle on top of the triangle. Hunter then said, "Ice-cream cone."

Mr. B. chuckled and replied, "That is not what I was looking for. I like it though. You are an out-of-the-box thinker."

The second incident was when Mr. B. was getting ready to leave our session. It was time for him to leave. Hunter did not want Mr. B. to leave. Hunter ran to Mr. B., who was now sitting on the floor and putting his shoes on. Hunter began to scream no and began to continuously hit Mr. B. Mr. B. stayed sitting quietly, proceeding to finish putting on his shoes while he asked, "Hunter, why are you so upset and hitting me?" Hunter did not answer. I went to Hunter and gently explained to Hunter that Mr. B. would return.

"Hunter, Mr. B. will be back." Hunter calmed down, and Mr. B. left. I was impressed with the degree of calm and patience that Mr. B. displayed. He was and still is a man I truly respect.

Hunter was still in his second year of school when my attorney filed the petition papers with the court on October 24, 2016. Included were eighteen supporting documents. This began the necessary investigative process of our home, our background, obtaining notarized letters of recommendation regarding our character and ability, and our primary care physician's confirmation that we could raise Hunter.

This was so foreign to us. It did require legwork. We had an extremely capable and likable adoption caseworker involved. We all loved and appreciated her. Life continued to be our normal busy: school, Mom to doctors, Hunter to therapies, and everyday household chores. Life was busy and evolving.

Imagine how I felt when I was praised for stepping up and into Hunter's classroom to help while they were looking for a teacher. They did not have a permanent teacher selected for the 2016–2017 school year, so I volunteered my time to make sure the temporary substitute had adequate support and that Hunter's educational needs were being met. It felt like I received appreciation, respect, and affirmation as they acknowledged that Hunter would continue to benefit and grow academically and behaviorally.

The following are excerpts from the letters of recommendation:

In September of 2015, we were in the process of moving from Interlochen to Tennessee. Amid the move, problems arose where we could not move into the new home for almost two weeks. The McClellans' immediately invited us and shared their home with us. During that time, I watched how much love they shared for Hunter and all that they were doing to help him just become a normal little boy. The improvements that we have seen in that little boy from being timid to running around happy and talking have been amazing. (Liz Brown)

The McClellan family are one of the few out there that I feel completely comfortable taking care of my kids. My kids adore them! They ask when they get to go there next. And when I had to be gone from home to take care of my sick mother, Mary took my kids for the night so that my husband could have a reprieve. They are wonderful people! (Cheyenne Long)

Their character is unmatched. They are a brilliant, kind, and patient couple with a deep-rooted faith unmatched by most. I have witnessed first-hand the love, time, energy, and resources that they have devoted to the development and growth of their great-grandson, Hunter. I have witnessed Hunter go from a timid, mostly non-verbal, underweight toddler to a robust, lean, well-mannered, talkative, and most importantly, joyful child—and all of this is due to the efforts of this amazing couple. (Everleigh Jacobson)

Finally, the report from Kay Barlow of Health and Human Services, which was lengthy, covered all aspects of Brian's and my individual histories, from childhood right up to the present. In addition, covered were financial strengths, character strengths, our bonds with each other, our job and academic history, and the services we were providing and planning for Hunter.

The following is one of her final statements:

> Brian and Mary are a very loving and committed couple. They communicate very well and are secure in their relationship and financial status. They have been providing care for Hunter for almost two years and show no sign of fatigue or diminished interest in raising a child.

I could go on and on with her comments. At our final adoption hearing, the judge asked if Kay Barlow had anything more to say. I recall that she said that it had been a pleasure to work with us and that she enjoyed our sense of humor as well. On May 3, 2017, the judge granted our adoption of Hunter.

I remember entering the courtroom feeling so unsure. As I reflect on that now, that is funny because, yes, it was a new process for us. Hunter was four years and three and a half months old. He was in the courtroom with us. The judge entered, we all stood, and he sat down and commented, "This won't take long." It took less than five minutes. We answered a couple of questions. He then said, "Granted." We said thank you and stood up.

Then Hunter turned and looked at the judge and said, "Tank oo."

That surprised me. I still wonder today if Hunter understood why he also said thank you. We went outside the courthouse, and our attorney took about twenty pictures of us together. Hunter was being silly.

CHAPTER 11

After the adoption, Hunter's class presented us with a framed picture of Hunter's hands the next school day. Above his hands were the words, "Worth the Wait." Below his handprints was the adoption date: May 3, 2017.

On May 18, 2017, I felt it wise to send a letter to our daughter Monica. Brian and I hoped it might be a letter of healing. We both signed the letter. I also included complete copies of all the letters of recommendation, the same notes the judge had also received.

Before sharing the letter, I would like the reader to see Monica's private message. Those most hurtful and untrue accusative words were: "You deceived, lied, and manipulated to get Hunter. If people knew what you did to MY family, they would be appalled!"

Those words cut my heart deeply. Of course, there was not any truth in them. I hoped that her words were merely a knee-jerk reaction to her pain. The pain that those words caused me has lessened through the years. Yet there is still a sense of both disappointment and despair.

The following is a replication of the letter we sent to our daughter Monica:

May 18, 2017

Dear Monica,

Last summer, dad and I realized that we had to see a lawyer to update our wills and complete the process, including Durable Power of Attorney, Medical Health Power, and establish a McClellans' Family Trust. While going through that process, we had intense discussions regarding "what if" scenarios and what would be best for our children and including Hunter, should something terrible happen to either of us in the immediate future. That took lengthy discussions and planning and review of legal documents. So, we put language and protections into place to protect and provide for Hunter and our children even if Hunter was not adopted.

We learned of Hunter's special health issues but did not know of all of them at that time. However, Hunter has specialists and therapists who have established a solid support base medically and emotionally. We know that Hunter needs them. As a result, it became apparent that it would not be best for Hunter to be pulled away from those services or the personal bonds he had established should anything happen to us in the immediate future.

So, we chose a primary and secondary guardian in that event. Our neighbors, Daren, and Everleigh, have become like family, are great parents, stable individuals, and love Hunter very much. They are willing to include him as a family in their life. In addition, they are ready to allow his biological family in his life. The secondary choice was Belinda because she and Hunter have bonded, and she, at this stage of Hunter's care required, is in the best position and location to provide him with what he needs for all his special needs.

I informed Deb of this and told her that it is not "cast in stone" and can be changed as situations change. You and Butch are busy and live in an area that cannot quickly provide Hunter with all the specialists and care at this time in his life. We are fortunate that God continues to bless and care for our health and that all our doctors provided the court with information stating that there is nothing that will prevent us from raising Hunter.

Hunter became Hunter S. McClellan on May the 3rd. It was a process that could have easily been derailed at any time. Hunter calls dad "Papa" and me "Mama." We want Hunter to know Deb as "mom" and have told her that. I have tried to post pictures and inform her of his progress and conditions as the pieces keep falling into place to help further him grow. This is to allow you and Deb to see how he is doing and what new hurdles he will face and conquer.

We established two bank accounts for Hunter. One is to receive his SSI, which will become his as a child of senior citizens. The other is his former SSI disability account. Hunter is the sole beneficiary. It is earmarked for his future educational or training needs. Again, we put strong language into our wills and trust to protect and distribute those funds to Hunter.

In January, Deb said things, out of anger and not the truth, including that it is over and we "win." It has always been what is best for a special need little boy who needed an advocate. Never was it to "win," but instead do what was best for Hunter.

God was so in this dream he gave me, and the devotional Dad had read that same day. Both showed us that we might have to adopt Hunter. We still hoped that Deb would agree to get the counseling she needed, get additional education, get her life together, and then provide support and guidance with Hunter. However, she declined, and three days after the dream, C.P.S. had Deb call to see if we would be willing to come to get Hunter and become his guardians. Still, we hoped that she would do the challenging work to get herself to parent well. However, we listened to the advice of Hunter's lawyer and chose to do the challenging work recommended by him and risk our family hating us. That has come true from your family.

It is a disappointment and saddens me that you seem to have forgotten how ethical your father and I are, how we would always do what was correct and legal, and how deeply we pray for God's guidance. I guess I can understand a little how you might forget, because you have not really seen us, walked our life with us regularly for years. Just a few visits, calls, and texts but not the daily seeing us live out our values. We are praying that God will provide healing.

Included are letters of recommendation to the court. I hope that will help you see truths that you have forgotten. How do we word this letter better to show you how we love you all but have to do the right thing? God made it clear what direction He wanted us to go with Hunter. Every time we questioned—we would either look at each other and state if God made it clear, then we should trust He will provide the strength and the resources, or someone or something would happen that could only have been God stepping in to keep us remembering what and who was important. What was and still is essential: our obedience and faith to and in God, who was and is important: First and foremost, Hunter—everyone else had to be next.

We are proud of your accomplishments, happy for you being able to begin your dream of living and retiring in the mountains, yet deeply saddened that you either are jumping to conclusions and perceptions that were not based on knowing the whole story and remember who we are. Hopefully, healing will begin.

Written with our deepest love,

Dad and Mom McClellan

Later, in 2017, we noticed that Hunter did not appear to be hearing. Hunter's school speech therapist had seen this as well. In addition, he might have been experiencing more seizures of some kind. We were not sure about the episodes. There were nights that he could not sleep well. I would hold Hunter in my arms while I was in our recliner rocker, and he would then drift off to sleep. Usually, his little arms and legs would jerk uncontrollably. Yet he would sleep through those jerking motions. Once, he was like that for the whole night. We contacted his neurologist. His neurologist felt that Hunter should go through a twenty-four-hour EEG at the Tennessee Children's Hospital. In April, he did so.

The Children's Resource Center kept Hunter busy by providing him toys to play with and movies to watch. Brian and I took turns going out for a break to rest or eat. Hunter, even though his head was wrapped in cloth bandages to hold on electrons, and he had wires dangling, was allowed to walk around. This EEG is where they saw that he had mild to moderate brain damage within the cognitive and language areas of the brain. However, they did not catch any seizure spikes.

We also approached Hunter's ENT doctors and asked Hunter to have him referred to the University of Tennessee to evaluate his hearing further. Tennessee's U of M accepted the referral. They evaluated his hearing at eight hundred decibels versus the five hundred decibels levels evaluated during his sedated ABR within the Tennessee Hearing Clinic. Tennessee U of M's testing confirmed that his left ear was profoundly deaf. Their audiologists felt that Hunter would benefit from a cochlear implant for his left ear.

I began researching the different implants and procedures involved, and I attended seminars from the various implant brands. I learned much. We then had to go through required levels of testing at the Tennessee U of M to determine eligibility in compliance with insurance requirements. Hunter became approved for the implant procedure. Once we received the insurance's approval, it was time for MRIs and CAT scans to narrow down the areas involved in the surgical procedure. Remember, we were also taking my mom to appointments and Hunter to gymnastics, speech therapy, and occupational therapy during all of this. We were one busy family. Still, we managed to have fun too. We raced outside, took Hunter on wagon rides, walked trails, and went for ice cream.

Classroom procedures smoothed out a bit from there on out. Speech and occupational therapies were beginning to make a noticeable difference in Hunter. Soon, he would be able to attend the Great Start Readiness program. I started the process and enrolled him in the Great Start Readiness program within the Blue Mountain Elementary School.

CHAPTER 12

I recall visiting the classroom first. Oh my, Ms. Em was intriguing, intimidating, and incredible, all rolled into one large package of intelligence! I was soon to learn how I could also learn from her. She was a joy! Both Hunter and I grew to love her dearly. She was a firm believer in children learning through play with little, gentle redirection and guidance. It works!

Hunter grew in kindness, listening skills, and creative, inventive techniques. One day, Hunter orchestrated and gathered his playmates to help and develop a catapult! What a great scientific experiment that was great fun for all. He impressed Ms. Em and this mama.

Another day, Hunter had an incident at school. His temperature rose quickly and went down to normal just as quickly. He began to stare into space for a few moments. We later learned that he was experiencing a focal seizure. He blacked out about four weeks later, fell, and hurt his nose. No one in his class had seen it happen. We were sure that it had to be a focal seizure.

November 2017, Hunter had his cochlear implant surgery. The week after his surgery, his school speech therapist came to our home. She brought so many cards of good wishes. His teachers and classmates had been busy making them for Hunter. That was a beautiful gift to Hunter and our hearts.

One month later, traveling in a slight snowstorm to the Tennessee U of M, we had the appointment to get it activated. What a day! So many emotions. The audiologists explained that we should not expect some big reaction like one often sees in news reports of babies hearing for the first time. We did not get that type of response. Yet it was joyously impressive!

The audiologists were programming the sensory processor while Hunter played with various toys. He was playing with Legos. Suddenly, he very quietly, without hesitation of play, stated, "Turn it down." We all had a great and happy chuckle! The team still had further testing and refining that they wished to do that day. So we left for lunch and a break.

We chose to go to the play area at a close-by mall. Hunter bonded with his processor the very same day! Usually, it takes about four to six weeks. Not for Hunter. What a blessing. In the months and years to follow, more therapies would be done to increase his ability to hear the high-frequency sounds and learn how to enunciate them. Five years later, we still work on it. However, he has made tremendous progress.

After the fall at school, Brian and I had a date in December to attend a company Christmas party. We had been there for a short while. It was an enjoyable evening with good conversations and food. However, it turned out to be a good thing that it was simply a short-lived party. As we were leaving, my phone rang. Our friend had volunteered for Hunter to stay with them. Everleigh's voice was full of panic. "Mary, Hunter just walked out to the kitchen where I am. He has a huge bump on his forehead, and he is not even crying! I do not know what happened. He was in the living room playing while the kids were watching a movie. What should I do? I do not want you to have to leave the party."

I replied, "Everleigh, we are in the car heading your way. We should be there shortly. Put a cold washcloth on the bump."

When we arrived, Hunter seemed not to feel any pain. It was a large bump, and he should have felt pain. However, he did not.

He had been sitting on the floor playing with Legos. He was near their marble fireplace hearth. He must have blanked out, fallen forward, and hit his head on the marble hearth. I was now sure that he had been experiencing more focal seizures.

We contacted Dr. Sam Dodge. I am so thankful that he did not immediately begin the Keppra. Hunter's two-month appointment with Tennessee U of M might not have been as productive and fun had he done so. At this appointment, they removed his hearing aid. Then they began to evaluate Hunter's ability to respond to directions. A visual board and a pointer stick were given to Hunter.

The audiologist explained to Hunter that they wanted him to use the pointer to point to the pictures when he heard them say the word. She placed the visual board in front of Hunter, handed him the pointer stick, placed the padded cover over her mouth, and began the process. For example, "Hunter, where is a hot dog?" Hunter correctly pointed to the hot dog. He could not say hot dog. What he called the hot dog was "haa."

One of the following choices generated hearty chuckles: "Hunter, where is a cupcake? Point to the cupcake." Hunter smiled, pointed at the cupcake, and said, "Happy day, cupcake!" Hunter associated cupcakes with birthday cake and birthday presents. Cupcakes made it a "happy day."

Once the visual directions were complete, the next step was to adjust the programming in his sensory processor. Hunter was to stack boxes as he heard a sound. At this stage and this age, it took visual coaxing to get any child to understand how and when to react to sounds when heard.

Our neurologist decided to put Hunter on Keppra for the seizures. Once again, I am glad that he had not started this before the Tennessee U of M visit. However, it was very shortly afterward.

Yikes! The side effects of that medication were horrendous! Hunter became angry and violent. This kind and compassionate little boy was now doing things like throwing tables and chairs, biting, and kicking. His behaviors were all over the place.

Fortunately, God put me in the position to help with the toddler nursery at church. The leader that day had an eight-year-old daughter who was on the same medication. Her daughter had similar reactions to the drug. Her doctor had recommended that she be on a regimen of vitamin B6.

The next day, I contacted Hunter's neurologist and received the same recommendation for Hunter. We had to order the special EZ Melts B6 50 mg online, as none of our stores or pharmacies could provide that specific form of B6. That vitamin was a Godsend! Commonly, positive responses happen in one to two weeks. We saw a positive response in just three days. We were so grateful, both for God's intervention and the patience and love that Ms. Em and the staff provided to our family.

Hunter was on Keppra for eight months when he started to experience large bumps. At first, we thought that he had gotten bitten by a bug or a bee. Then the spots became huge over his face and up and down his arms. Off to the walk-in clinic! They thought it might be a bite of some kind but could not tell for sure. I am a type A personality and love to research possibilities and solutions. So I researched Keppra's side effects. I saw that hives could be a side effect.

Poor Hunter. He was so miserable! The pharmacist confirmed that it was a rare side effect. Why it took eight months to begin, no one could say. That medication also contributed to Hunter's inability to remain calm. Once we discontinued the drug, it took about a week to heal his skin and another two weeks to calm his little brain further. He continues to be off seizure medication. Yes, there are times that he has a quick focal seizure. To date, they still have not been able to catch one on an EEG.

Having the strong, compassionate, and patient Great Start Readiness staff surrounding our Hunter and us was a true blessing. We will never forget them and forever cherish their compassion.

CHAPTER 13

In May 2018, we traveled to Ohio to visit Uncle Devan and Aunt Belinda. We were also going to see their children and fit in a trip to the Children's Museum of Ohio. The museum is the world's largest children's museums. It had now been two years since we had visited the museum.

Jerry and Kendra had stopped by to visit. Later, Devan, Belinda, Kendra, Jerry, Brian, Hunter, and I went to the museum. I had decided to bring Hunter's Mini Mouse, for his cochlear sensory processor, along with us. Boy, was I glad that I had! That Hunter! He remembered the museum. As soon as check-in stamped our tickets, Hunter took off running! That entertained our gang. They wondered where Hunter was heading. As I ran after Hunter, I said, "I know where he is heading!" I kept talking to Hunter through the Mini Mouse. "Hunter, stop! Wait for me!" We ended up taking turns chasing Hunter down. However, I was correct. Hunter went right to the floor where the cars were. There he could take off and put on car tires. I still am amazed that his memory was so great after two years. It was about two floors up to reach the cars. He kept us busy, and, like before, we had great fun and challenges keeping up with Hunter.

Hunter has a way of unintentionally making life enjoyable. He did not fail that weekend either. Uncle Devan had vehicles in his possession: cars, trucks, tractors, lawnmowers, and a quad. Belinda decided it might be fun to let Hunter sit with her on the recreational vehicle. Of course, Hunter was all for doing that. Then she gave our five-year-old Hunter a lesson in how to steer the quad. Belinda became aware of how Hunter would drive and was able to quickly redirect their path. Devan's daughter, Catherine, came for a visit. I am unsure who decided it, but Catherine agreed to get on the quad and invited Hunter. Belinda was in the process of telling Catherine what to watch for with Hunter when—crash! They crashed right into the corner of their home, where the gas line went into their home. Oh no!

It was excellent that their fire department was about five blocks away. They had to come and check out things. Hunter happened to be extremely interested in fire trucks and firefighters. He was happily excited! Gratefully, nothing major happened.

Belinda explained that Hunter liked fire trucks and firefighters to one of the crew. She asked, "Do you think we could get a picture of you together with Hunter and me?" Such a nice man to agree. We have the loveliest picture of Belinda holding Hunter, standing in front of a fire truck with one firefighter. What an exciting day. Poor Catherine! I do not think she knew what to do and felt so bad. It was not her fault.

Overall, we had lots of fun and had a great visit. We met Kendra's Jerry for the first time. He and Kendra would later marry. He was and is a kind and considerate gentleman. We are pleased to say he is in our family.

CHAPTER 14

June 2018 was so much fun! Hunter's sister Annie and brother Alden came and stayed with us for five days. We filled each day with laughter. Occasionally, there were tears. The tears were usually from Alden. Alden had a weakness for the slightest minor injury. I mean *slight*! If Alden had a minimal abrasion, he would immediately panic and cry uncontrollably. He was eight years old. I often told him that he was going to be all right. Alden's crying would often—fortunately not always—trigger Hunter to begin screaming out of fear. Hunter did not understand what was happening.

One afternoon, we were outside playing when Alden abrased his elbow. It was a minor scrape and did not even draw blood. I was sitting on the deck watching them play and have fun together. Alden approached me crying, not as loud this time, and showed me his injury. I looked at Alden and said, "Alden, you did not even bleed. It is going to be all right. Just be brave and go play." He did do.

Hunter and Annie were playing with his little red wagon. They were taking turns pulling each other around the driveway circle. All three children also played in the sandbox. They would switch up what play they would do. Sometimes it was also walking in the woods or riding the bikes. Alden had recently learned how to pedal his bike and had brought it with him.

The next day, accident-prone Alden once again obtained a slight scrape while we were driving on our way to the beach. Not crying, he promptly began to inform me what had happened. He proudly said, "See? I was brave."

I replied, "Yes, you were. I am proud of you." We spent the day at the beach and visited the sand dunes. We usually stopped and had ice cream on the way home. It was a good day.

We had a little pond down in our valley. It was a fun little hike down to the pond. One day, Hunter, Annie, and I went down by the pond. We saw little tadpoles and tiny frogs in the pond. It was muddy around the pond. Both children had fun stomping in the mud and trying to catch a tadpole. Alden would not come down to the pond. He did not like it or feel safe there. Alden had anxieties and sensory issues going on. He would stay up the hill and play or ride his bike.

Another day, we decided to go to the Brown Township Park. They had a splash pad that was so much fun. I put Hunter's special covering and magnet onto his sensory processor and removed his hearing aid. He could now play in the water with his special processor attachments. I removed his hearing aid because it could not get wet.

It was fantastic to see the three running, laughing, and playing so well together. Kudos to Annie and Alden because it was still tough to understand Hunter's words. All was going very well—until leaving the park when Alden began to scream. Oh my! Such screaming!

Hunter began to panic. I was now dealing with two upset children. Alden would not or could not explain. We got to the car. I buckled a screaming Hunter into the vehicle. I got the other two in and buckled. *Finally,* Alden told me that a fly had landed on him.

That did it for me! I had it! I did indeed (although I should not have) yell at Alden, "Stop this screaming! You are scaring Hunter, and that is not OK!" I would not leave the parking lot until Alden stopped crying. Finally, I simply stated, "I had planned to take you all for ice cream again. If this crying does not stop, that is not happening." Excellent, not really; that statement immediately stopped Alden's crying. It took a few more moments for Hunter to calm down. Whew! That was work! Hurray for ice cream!

It is now near the end of their visit with us. Annie and Hunter often sat at our clavi nova and attempt to make music together. Alden usually played a game, played with toys, or watched cartoons.

We all decided to go outside again. Alden was riding his bike, Annie and Hunter were playing with the wagon, and I was either sitting on the deck or walking in our woods. Suddenly, I heard a scream and crying. Annie ran to get me. Alden had fallen off his bike. He had been riding too fast, causing his bike to go off the edge of our paved drive. The bike had tipped, causing Alden to fall. He had hit his knee on the driveway hard enough to scrape it badly and draw blood. This time, his reaction was justified. Alden would not get up or move. I asked him to stay while I got supplies to clean and bandage his scrape. I was proud of Alden; he cried quietly and became a bit calmer. I took a picture of his knee, cleaned it, and then bandaged his knee. Of course, I contacted Sophia and sent her a picture of Alden's knee.

When Sophia called, she and I discussed the events of the week. We both decided that it was time for the kids to come home. We agreed to meet them halfway. Even though there were definite times of chaos, it had been a great visit.

Our grandson, Paul, was soon to have an open house. It was a celebration of his graduation from high school. Brian, Hunter, Mom, and I all attended the graduation. Belinda and Devan also were able to come. I loved seeing all the pictures of Paul from early childhood through the years. It was good to see him. His sister Kenzie also was able to attend. It was good to see her. However, she acted a little awkward around us. I understood why she was feeling uncomfortable. We had also attended and supported her when she graduated from high school. She had received a large scholarship to attend. The scholarship was for soccer. She was good at soccer. However, she did not put in the effort to practice before her college session began, nor did she practice as required when there. Eventually, Kenzie simply walked out one day and never returned. So she felt a bit guilty. It did leave her dad, our son Colton, with a balance to repay the college. Kenzie was struggling with her emotions. She felt that her dad did not like her anymore. I simply told her that yes, he did. Eventually, she approached him and hugged him. Their relationship is strained still today.

Mom enjoyed the opportunity to see family and get out of the house. Even with her walker, we were able to make her comfortable. Hunter entertained everyone. He loved looking at the pictures of Paul. Hunter could easily entertain others merely by how or what food he would eat. His method of eating could also be entertaining. Hunter thinks a hamburger is only a hamburger if it consists of a bun with catsup and mustard. It is still true of him today.

CHAPTER 15

We had our next McClellans' annual weekend get-together. Our time together was filled with laughter, food, fun games, catching up with one another, trips to the beach and park, and late nights just chilling out. This was the year that I announced that we would take a break from hosting the get-togethers. Yes, it was fun.

However, it was tiring, and Mom was beginning to fall more. I had to take care of her more. Near the end of our get-together, I got the gang's attention and made the announcement. I remember people looking a little surprised, and a hush fell over the room. Then Brian's sister, Tootsie, looked around and asked, "So who's going to host next time?"

I then stated that we felt that we needed to and hoped to spend time traveling and visiting our family one on one. I then said, "You know that you may visit anytime. You do not necessarily have to visit with us. You may go sightseeing and simply stay here. I hope that you all feel like you can." That ended the conversation. I had caught everyone off guard.

As I stated, my mom's health continued to worsen. We had to call an ambulance a couple of times. Once, it was early in the morning. We asked for no sirens because that would have frightened Hunter. She had fallen in her bathroom and hit her head on the door casing. The impact was right over her right eye. Somehow, she also managed to fall over on the bathtub and badly bruise her ribs. The ambulance crew did not take her to the hospital. It was later we learned that she had broken one of her ribs.

She had previously fallen and broken her right hip. We had dealt with that earlier. This was yet another fall. When I say we were a busy household, we were. Many responsibilities fell onto my shoulders alone: taking Hunter to appointments, Mom to appointments, church, planning trips, get-togethers, taking Hunter to Professor Qwibli's camp, and simply everyday household chores. I was wearing out.

I had asked Mom to consider visiting my sister, Paula, for just a couple of weeks to give me a break. Mom did not want to do that. She was concerned that Paula's bathroom facilities would not work for her. Paula was also concerned. In addition, Paula, for years, had been an emotionally unstable individual. I would not have even suggested Mom go there. However, I needed a break, and Paula was doing better. Mom did not end up going.

It was the Fourth of July. Hunter had not yet attended a Fourth of July parade. I decided to take him to one in Blue Mountain. We were able to park blocks away. He and I decided to sit under a tree outside the open space by Mineral Park and watch the parade. His little warrior friend, Carrie Lyn, was also there with her family. I had not noticed that they were directly across from us. Her mom, Alexis, saw us first and invited us to sit with them. It was nice to watch Hunter and Carrie Lyn together.

Hunter was shy and a bit hesitant. He was not sure what to think about the different sounds and parade activities. He was slow to realize that he could pick up the candy and the necklaces thrown toward them. This parade is where I first met Alexis's mom, Carrie. Oh my, does that lady have energy! She would run right up to a vehicle and request the candy, necklace, or whatever freebie was about to be thrown. Then she would quickly bring it over to

Hunter and Carrie Lyn. Carrie was a hoot then and still is today. However, she is also the best "grammy" and kindest individual.

Once the parade ended, Hunter, Carrie Lyn, her parents, and I crossed the street to attend the little carnival. The kids had fun going on the rides. It was nice for them to be able to do that together. Yes, it was a busy day. It was a pleasant change from taking care of appointments or household chores.

Brian and Hunter had fun water fights between the Fourth of July and the eighteenth of July. They were usually on our back deck, splashing water out of the little toddler pool or turning the hose on each other. Hunter continually lined his cars and trucks up in progression, either on the floor or on the back of the couch. It was common for Hunter to go downstairs into the Cave and watch a movie. Sometimes, he would line up his Disney characters and tell them to watch the movie. There was always something fun happening between Brian and Hunter or Hunter and me. Sometimes it was the three of us. Hunter still did not go anywhere in our home unless one of us were with him or near him.

Mom fell again on July 18, 2018. This time she bruised both of her eyes and severely injured her knees. She did end up in the hospital for that fall. I called my brother, Eugene, who lived in Montana, to let him know of her fall. I also called my sister Maria and told her about Mom's fall. Eugene decided to come to see Mom. He had not seen Mom or his children in years. He thought that this might be a wise time to make the trip.

I had informed the hospital social worker that I did not want her to go back home. I felt that she had been falling too much. She needed more care than I could provide. Plus, I was simply tired. The hospital decided to discharge Mom to a nursing home facility.

I took her to that facility. Arriving there, the exterior looked well cared for. I was hopeful. However, it turned out to be a very unsafe facility. As the director walked us to what was to be Mom's room, I noticed dangerous hallways—narrow hallways filled with large equipment. The director stopped at the nursing station and introduced us to the aide or nurse, just across from what was to be Mom's room. She took us into what was to be her room. It was tiny. There were no bedside tables, no closets, and it had three little cots bumper to bumper.

Two women were in the room, uncovered and almost naked. Their bodies were like skeletons. She then sent us down to a waiting room and asked me to wait for her return. I sat there and decided that I would not leave Mom there. I told Mom, "Let's get up and go out." I stopped by the nurse's station outside of what would have been Mom's room and said, "We are leaving. I am not leaving my mother here! It is unsafe."

The nurse must have taken the back route to the manager's office. He was there already talking with her. The manager came out and attempted to convince me to leave Mom there. As the manager had me against a wall, she said, "This is a wonderful place. We all love each other. We are a family. We take loving care of each other."

I simply stated, "I am not leaving my mom here. We are leaving." I did have to sign a paper. The manager did not know that I had experience working in a nursing home facility. I could identify the errors and dangers. I did report them to the state of Tennessee. Later, I received a thirty-three-page report containing infractions. The irony is that a facility may receive a citation. However, those with violations are given a specific amount of time to fix the violations. The state inspectors will later conduct a follow-up. If the infraction still exists, they merely receive another citation. The process continues. My brother, Eugene, was happy that I had brought Mom home. Still, it required more work, even though I did receive in-home care for Mom.

My anxiety and workload were increasing. I had begun to investigate an assisted-living facility for her. Unfortunately, she did not earn enough to get into an assisted-living facility. I made phone calls and connected with the Area of the Aging. Plus, I had in-home assistants coming in one to two times a week to help her shower and change and clean her and her room. Still, she was getting worse, and I was exhausted.

One day, I received a call from the Area of the Aging. They found two assisted-living homes that would be willing to put her on a list. Then I also put her on the waiting list for the Brookside. One exhausting day, I stopped by the one assisted-living facility merely to see it. I was emotionally exhausted and just started to talk about who we were—how we adopted our special needs great-grandson and how Mom needed so much more help. I broke out in tears and apologized. The lady asked, "Have you talked with Nikki yet?"

"Who is Nikki?" I replied.

She said, "Nikki is my sister and is in charge. She could arrange something for you. I will talk to her."

I still had not heard from Nikki. However, it was now time for Hunter to begin kindergarten.

CHAPTER 16

We did the usual fun things during summer. We had gone to the beach, played outside, went visiting, had our annual McClellan get-together, gardened, worked on learning to ride a bicycle, and added in an event at Professor Qwibli's. So much fun and laughter.

Hunter was really into Pete the Cat. Hunter wanted to "rock red shoes" like Pete the Cat in kindergarten. Proudly, he stood tall, crossed his arms, and smiled as he posed for a picture of him in his red shoes. Hunter looked cool.

About three weeks had passed when I received a call from the Area of the Aging. They had found that one assisted-living space was willing to reduce their rates. It was the facility that I had visited. This meant that Mom might be able to get into an assisted-living facility.

I went to talk with Nikki. She very kindly agreed to take Mom in but not until sometime in December. She wanted a deposit to hold the room. I shared the information with Brian. He said, "Let us do it. Let us take the money out and make the deposit ourselves." So I did just that.

Mom knew that we were looking into an assisted-living arrangement. She knew that it was a process. Of course, she was not happy with that. Even though it was she who had told me often, "If I ever get too much for you to manage, I want you to put me into a nursing home." I went to Mom and informed her that they had made progress, and it looked like an opening would be available soon. I did not provide specific details. She needed to take this all in. I knew that she needed to soak up this information.

During the summer of 2018, we made an appointment with Dr. Woolery. We were and are fortunate to have a psychiatrist who also has a medical degree. Dr. Woolery saw Hunter again in October 2018. He previously did the initial examination and testing: physical, developmental, emotional, and mental. It was Dr. Woolery who determined that Hunter had the following diagnoses: ASD (on the spectrum of autism), OCD (obsessive-compulsive disorder), FAS (fetal alcohol syndrome), ADHD (attention deficit hyperactivity disorder), and unspecified anxiety. Dr. Woolery stated that he did not like the effects of medications routinely given for individuals on the spectrum or who had ADHD.

He explained that he found that a compound of Guanfacine, usually used to treat blood pressure, was highly effective in treating ASD and ADHD. However, it would require Hunter to receive a base EKG to ensure no irregularities in his heart.

He also recommended Hunter take a particular omega-3 supplement. He urged the brand name CoraOmega3. He stated that it was the purest form and immediately went directly to the brain. It helped to heal the brain. This form of CoraOmega3 was also in a kid-friendly format. It was a creamy liquid that tasted much like orange sherbet. It was this CoraOmega3 that contributed to healing Hunter's mild to moderate brain damage. Remember, we only knew that he had been born hearing impaired, had been in the NIC unit for eight days, had seizures, and had been diagnosed with hypoxic ischemic encephalopathy.

We had a new IEP and support team in place for Hunter. Hunter's first three weeks were stressful for both Hunter and me. The office would call and ask me to pick up Hunter. He either cried, screamed, ran out of the classroom, or was noncompliant. It was then that I requested we receive daily reports of Hunter's behaviors and accomplishments. His anxieties triggered Hunter's outbursts. In addition, he had only been off the Keppra about four weeks. He also had only been on the CoraOmega3 about three weeks.

I was grateful that Dr. Woolery provided the school with a letter including Hunter's diagnoses and recommendations. Hunter's anxieties came from loud sounds, especially fire alarms, bathroom doors had to be open, and he had to be near us when he was at home. The school tried to separate him from the other students, thinking he would be less distracted or less of a distraction. Neither worked for Hunter. He was antisocial and primarily nonverbal. He did engage in echolalia. You can imagine what a challenge he must have been for the school staff. Indeed, they tried their best.

He had the best kindergarten teacher, Mr. Hunt. He was patient, excellent in every aspect, and still says that he learned how to instruct children even more through Hunter. I remember being in tears the last time I had to bring him home. What to do? Well, we sent him right back to school.

They would take Hunter for a quick walk when he became agitated. Thankfully, the janitor knew Hunter and me. He understood our story. I am so grateful that he informed me that they walked Hunter for as long as thirty minutes! That did not accomplish getting Hunter to acclimate to the system. It only provided Hunter his preferred activity.

I then spoke with his special education teacher, who was also the coordinator of his IEP. and informed her, "Misty, I have been made aware of the length of time that Hunter is on walks. That is not acceptable. It is to be no longer than five minutes. You cannot pull the wool over my eyes!"

Afterward, they stopped taking Hunter on walks. Instead, they began to send him into the office. Hunter was to sit in a chair. Whew! Really? That also did not get him to acclimate to the classroom environment. I had serious conversations with the team. Eventually, I periodically showed up and sat in the hall outside of the classroom. My presence had a calming effect on Hunter.

My presence helped Hunter adjust to the routines. Eventually, interrupted routines did not cause Hunter to become upset. Often, it was because he knew I was there. I was his security blanket. The team and I weaned him from requiring my presence to make him feel safe and secure.

The time was getting closer to telling my mother that an opening was available for her to move to assisted living. After Thanksgiving, I let her know that she could move in on December 15. I then informed Mom that I had asked if she could wait until after Christmas, and they had agreed.

Mom was bitter and angry. She contacted my sister Paula and asked her to come to the house. She wanted Paula to help her sort out papers and pictures that she had kept over the years. Mom was so angry that she gave Paula all her photographs, which contained our family's historical photos. I kept quiet about that. Yet inside, I was sad. I was sad because I knew that Paula would not retain them or share them with her siblings.

Those were hard days for Mom and me. Mom would often angrily say, "My Christmas gift to you is my leaving!" Hard, hard days full of heartaches and tension. I tried so hard to make things easier for her. I followed her wishes to allow Pula to take whatever and pack what things she wanted to bring to assisted living. Those were tough weeks!

Hunter participated in field trips and class activities. He had a blast and made excellent friends. However, he still had anxieties. Through the summer, we helped him to "boss" them down. Sometimes he willingly allowed us to let him boss them down. Other times, it was not the case.

On one trip to the Tennessee U of M, it was time for him to go to the bathroom. He refused to go into bathrooms that had a fire alarm. It was time for Hunter to use the bathroom. He had to go. The waiting room was full of people. I took Hunter's hand and told him that we were going to the bathroom. Immediately, he began to scream, lie down on the floor, and refuse. I took his hand and took him into the bathroom. Hunter fought me, screaming and crying the entire time.

Once in the bathroom, I reminded him that I was right there with him. I explained that we should boss down that fire alarm as Dr. Woolery had instructed. I explained that fire alarms were for emergencies, and I knew what to do. I went on to explain that I would protect him if there was an emergency.

I am sure that everyone could hear me explaining these things to Hunter. Hunter did become calm and walked calmly out of the bathroom. He never did that again. Through the years, Hunter's anxieties changed. Sometimes it was the drains in the road or bathroom floors or simply a new sound. Does he still have anxieties? Yes, but they are shorter-lived and manageable.

CHAPTER 17

In June 2019, Hunter and I attended my nephew Blane Clouse's wedding. They were married at a beautiful church in Blue Mountain, Tennessee. Hunter looked so cute in his little dark blue suit. He wore a vest instead of a suit coat. He had a light pink shirt on and wore a tie with a dark blue and pink pattern. He was one handsome and happy little boy. The wedding was beautiful.

All felt the joy. Hunter and I went to the reception hall and waited for the wedding party to enter. I laughed when they entered. The whole party, parents included, entered dancing. Each couple made their own special modern dance moves. Even the parents joined in. Blane and his wife ceremonially again dedicated their life and marriage to God at the reception. It was a beautiful moment. What a wonderful day.

Brian, Hunter, and I decided to visit his sister and her husband. Brian has two sisters. Brian's sister was lovingly nicknamed "Tootsie," and it has always stuck. She sure is a remarkable young lady. Brian was only eighteen years old when she was born.

Her husband, Mike, received a nickname. His name is "Mongo." We do not know how, when, or why he received that name. He is well loved by all. We, however, call him Mike. Mike loves to work with engines. He has classic cars he is rebuilding. He also has two or three tractors. Later that day, Mike gave Hunter a ride on one of the tractors. That made Hunter's day! When Hunter gets excited, he begins moving his hands in his autistic mannerisms. Often, he also will just wiggle in delight.

Later that day, we saw Brian's other sister, Joy, and her husband, Jonathon. We had a lovely visit that day. It was nice to see them all.

We took Hunter on his first canoe trip down the Grand River to the Lake Tennessee outlet. It was a beautiful day on July 21. Hunter sat in the middle of the canoe. Occasionally, Hunter would lay down in the canoe while holding onto the middle seat. The river was full of canoers and tubers that day. We heard, "Hello, McClellans!" That caught us off guard, and we looked around. We did not recognize them immediately. However, we soon spotted our neighbors, the Steele family. They were all in one large tube. They had three children, all under the age of seven. We said our hellos and went our separate ways down the river. It was such a fun experience—one that Hunter loved!

We put Hunter into a weeklong camp at Professor Qwibli's that summer. He did well there. He still was quite autistic and developmentally delayed. However, he grew in abilities, made friends, and had a blast! Socially, it was an excellent experience for him.

Summer ended, and it was time for Hunter to start first grade. In addition to school, Hunter's schedule included gymnastics, speech therapy, and occupational therapy.

We met his first-grade teacher, Ms. Battlefield, at the open house. It was an opportunity for the teacher to meet her students and their parents. I approached her to ask a question. She kept walking. Eventually, I asked her, "Have you learned information about who Hunter is? Do you know his history?"

She curtly and quickly replied, "I've been told that he's intelligent." Then she continued walking around the room. It irritated me because we were the only ones in the room with her. A couple of parents had just begun to enter the classroom.

Hunter and all students received their assessment to check for the summer slide. The staff found that Hunter did not have the summer slide as most students did. He both maintained and excelled.

His first-grade teacher was not a kind teacher. One day, as I dropped Hunter off at his locker, I noticed a young classmate sitting at a table. He was working on a paper and had a question. His question must have been about a new topic from the day before. His teacher turned, briefly looked at him, turned away again, and stated, "Just do what I told you yesterday!" She then continued distributing papers at the table.

A parent told me their child had said, "She's a good teacher, but she's insulting!" Hunter had a paraprofessional who was to tutor him from 10:00 a.m. throughout the day. Occasionally, when Hunter attended his school's OT or ST sessions, the paraprofessional would help other children. Eventually, the staff would pull Hunter's paraprofessional to work with other children. These children did not have an IEP. The staff's decision to pull her from Hunter was a violation of his IEP. The paraprofessional was explicitly to work with Hunter.

Yes, we could have hired a lawyer, gone to court, and won the battle. As Dr. Woolery pointed out, "You would win the battle. However, you would lose the war. You cannot be at school to monitor what is happening. The staff would not comply or work with Hunter as they should."

At that point, I merely kept observing what was happening within the school. I saw Hunter's teacher purposely choose not to speak with me as I waited to address her treatment of him. Hunter and I had returned from Hunter's hearing specialist, caring and working on Hunter's sensory processor. His teacher had already given the class instructions on the papers she had distributed. When Hunter and I entered the room, she handed Hunter his assignment, sat him at a different table far away from the other students, and proceeded to go from student to student and discuss their progress.

Hunter was looking confused and rightfully so. This was unacceptable! I wanted to question his teacher, "Why did you merely hand Hunter a paper and provide no direction?" However, she would not come to me as I patiently waited for ten minutes. She glanced over her shoulder and ignored my presence! I did leave that day. I did not address the problem with the principal. I knew that it would not accomplish any positive results. The principal also had been in noncompliance with Hunter's IEP.

One day, Ms. Battlefield sent me a message. The message stated that "Hunter is standing in the middle of the room screaming. We are trying to get ready to go to lunch."

I replied, "What is he screaming or saying?" She did not answer me immediately. I decided to call the school office. I asked to speak with Misty to find out what was going on in Hunter's classroom. Misty returned my call and said that Ms. Battlefield was busy and could not reply to my response.

Finally, Ms. Battlefield did reply, "He isn't saying anything."

When Hunter came home, I asked him why he was screaming. Hunter shared that another student was hitting one of the other students. Hunter gave me the boy's name. It happened to be the name of the boy who had physically been beating on Hunter before. Hunter was frightened. He could not find words to explain. Ms. Battlefield should have asked the students to wait; she should have gotten to Hunter's eye level and asked him what was happening. She did not. I knew that it was time to pull Hunter and homeschool him.

I informed Dr. Woolery of the incident and my decision. His only concern was Hunter's access to socialization. I stated that we were active in our church, Hunter could go to gymnastics, and we would see that he got socialization in other areas.

I drafted the legally acceptable letter informing the school of our decision. I copied every team member on his IEP and the appropriate school staff members. Each letter was in an envelope, sealed and individually addressed. On Friday, I contacted the school and told them that we would be picking Hunter up from school. Hunter knew that we were going to pick him up from school. He did not know why.

We walked into the school. Brian went to Hunter's locker, I handed letters out to the appropriate individuals, and requested Hunter's medications and hearing aid supplies. Brian and Hunter cleaned out his locker, and we walked out.

When we returned home, we told Hunter that we would do school at home from now on. I had known that I might someday have to teach Hunter. I had purchased college textbooks on ABA (applied behavior analysis) therapy and read books on autism. I had been a good student. I knew that I could teach Hunter.

Hunter immediately loved homeschooling. He created his version of a school cheer! It usually went as follows: "See Hunter do homeschool. In first grade. But I love homeschooling! Yay!"

We had purchased a little green table. Green was one of Hunter's favorite colors. The table was a sturdy table and adjustable in height. We hung a map of the United States of America above the table. The chairs were not adjustable. However, the chairs could hold up to a three-hundred-pound individual.

I had purchased grade-appropriate school materials. We had workbooks for reading, general language arts, math, geography, science, and social studies. Hunter and I worked side by side. This allowed me to also work on his proper enunciations.

He was able to stay focused. He had opportunities to express questions or make silly comments. Even the stupid words were opportunities for him to learn. In addition, he had the freedom to make his autistic vocalizations. This was an opportunity not available to him within the public school system. He grew in academic abilities. He succeeded in confidence. Then he began to understand things like what, where, when, and why. He also began recognizing and identifying pronouns. His favorite subjects were science, geography, and social studies.

We chose to do fun things together like getting our hands all sticky, making homemade bread, working outside, cleaning up the floor of our woods, following the neighbor's chickens, and playing outside. One day, on April 5, 2020, we decided to take our break on our deck. Hunter and Brian chose to have hot chocolate. I decided to have hot tea. Brian had asked Hunter, "What is Mama going to drink?"

Hunter's reply, "Pee!" A note here: Hunter could not hear all sounds well. To Hunter, the word tea sounded like pee. We all had a chuckle. Even Hunter realized that he had made a mistake. Soon, we were going back and forth, teasing and correcting Hunter.

On April 10, 2020, we went outside exploring. Brian opened our grill. He had not covered it before winter. He found inside it a nest of baby squirrels. Hunter said, "That doesn't belong there."

Papa replied, "We are going to have baby squirrels for lunch."

I said, "No. That wouldn't be very nice."

Hunter answered, "No, that's yucky!" Then we looked around and found a nest of baby squirrels. The nest was at the base of a tree. We hoped that the mama squirrel was somewhere nearby.

In April 2020, we went bac to Tennessee U of M for Hunter's assessments. Hunter's speech pathologist was pleased with his results. After six months of receiving homeschooling, the Tennessee U of M testing showed that Hunter had gained eighteen months of ability. He was no longer severely delayed. He now was moderately delayed.

Two days later, we decided to walk into our subdivision. The coronavirus had been keeping most people isolated. People chose to stay home. They would not even go outside into their yards. There was so much fear within our society. Yes, even the government was placing restrictions on the public. We ventured out to wave and said, "Hi, neighbors." Not one neighbor reacted to our hello. On our way back, a neighbor had driven into the subdivision. He did stop, and we had a friendly conversation.

We took road trips and shared a little bit of local history. Sometimes, we would share our experiences in certain areas. All these adventures provided different firsthand learning experiences. They gave opportunities for Hunter to mature.

We loved the month of April 2020. We cleared in the woods, worked on the garden, and pulled away leaves. Hunter loved pulling the work trailer. These activities filled our recess and early-evening times.

One day, Brian was working in our blueberry patch. Hunter came to get me and asked, "What is Papa doing?"

I replied, "I do not know. Let us see what he is doing." We found Brian near the blueberry patch. Brian had earphones on with music blasting. Hunter thought that Papa looked funny. Brian also had old, outdated CDs tied to strings. I thought that was odd. "Brian, what are you doing with those?"

He replied, "I am going to tie them onto the blueberry bushes. That will keep the birds away."

In May 2020, we had Max and Sherry Landis' children over for a sleepover. As usual, we played outside, laughed, and did crafts. Later the girls had great fun having a bubble bath in our Jacuzzi.

On May 27, 2020, I posted on Facebook:

> I am getting real! This isolation is getting to me!!! It is getting to many. Please find things to be grateful for. Hang on tight to each other and to God I am being real because I get things done each day: homeschool, check on mom and family, go to appointments, treasure my time within God's word, yet I am sad. Sad for connection, sad watching distancing, and yet grateful to connect when opportunities present. There are not enough

words to express my feelings. Hang in friends. Love you all.

That same day, I shared how Hunter and I have our good-night rituals. Our conversations were like the following: Hunter would say, "I love you, Mama."

One night, I replied, "I love you too. Why do you love me?"

Hunter's reply was "Because you're in my heart."

We often had the Landis girls over that summer. It was always a fun time. Brian, Hunter, and I had spent time at the beach and on local road trips. The coronavirus contributed to our state locking down the right to visit our family members in assisted-living facilities or nursing homes. We had not been able to see my mom, Abigale. I would call her or FaceTime her. My sister Maria wanted to visit Mom. The Brookside had recently set up "window visitation."

We arranged for Maria to come. Maria, her daughter Hanna, Hanna's daughters, Hunter, and I visited Mom. Mom loved seeing all of us. However, it was hard for her because she could not hear Maria on her phone. The staff brought a portable landline phone to Mom and gave us the number. Maria was then able to talk to Mom. Mom enjoyed seeing us all. She especially enjoyed watching her young great-great-grandchildren playing.

CHAPTER 18

The remainder of the summer of 2020 was busy with trips to the beach. We would play outside, exploring the trails and paths on our five acres of land. Brian and Hunter would have a gym session within our great room. Hunter was not coordinated. Brian would take the time with Hunter to illustrate how to throw or catch a ball. They would giggle back and forth. Brian would tell Hunter, "Keep your eye on the ball."

Hunter decided it was his turn to teach Papa how to catch the ball. His comments were comical. "Watch me again. Watch this way. Ready? Catch it!" Of course, Hunter inserted and demonstrated positions with his hands and arms while making those comments. Hunter was often very comical to watch.

One day, we decided to walk onto one of the nearby piers. It was mildly breezy. Brian held Hunter's hand as they walked. They saw seagulls landing onto the dock. They watched them take flight. Brian said to Hunter, "Watch the bird. It is getting ready to land."

When it landed, Hunter said, "He's a silly bird."

From there, we continued taking our road trip. We found ourselves taking more road trips and avoiding people. The coronavirus was impacting so many people. Brian was especially concerned about catching the virus. I was cautious but not concerned. Only God knows when it is our time to join Him in heaven.

We next headed out to explore the Apache area. There is a lookout bluff that overlooks Lake Tennessee. There are about one hundred steps to climb up to the top. At the top, there is a set of binoculars to look out over the waters There are also two old benches to rest on. Once Hunter sat on a bench, he stated, "We made it! We are sitting down on the old seat." (Hunter still was talking in fragmented sentences.) The sky was beautifully clear and blue. The clouds were few and simply bright white.

That summer, Brian decided to scrape and paint our front deck railing. Occasionally, Brian would hand Hunter a large strip of paint. He would tell Hunter that it was Hunter's "junk mail." Hunter enjoyed watching his Papa.

Hunter certainly has a sense of humor. He and Brian like to watch shows like *Just for Gags* or *America's Funniest Home Videos* together. In one episode, a mother had changed her mind. I have no idea about what or why. However, Hunter began laughing and said, "Mama changed her mind. Mama changed her mind. That is dumb! Dumb means that is silly." I was videoing Hunter's excited comments and actions. Suddenly, Hunter turned and saw that I had my phone and said, "Mama's got a sneaky camera!"

We did not attend the Fourth of July 2020 parade. Instead, we decided to go to the beach. Crowds of people were at the beach. We were surprised because it was just a little past 8:00 p.m. We managed to find a spot away from any groups of people. Hunter was able to play in the water with his little floating tube. Later, he found a long piece of driftwood and used it as his boat. It was a peaceful, fun evening. We left about 10:00 p.m. to return home. On the way home, we were able to see fireworks.

My left knee had needed surgery. My surgeon rescheduled my surgery because of the COVID restrictions. I finally had that done on July 20, 2020.

Summer was over. Hunter and I were doing our second-grade homeschooling together again. Life consisted of our standard routines. Normal for us was wake up, get ready for the day, Brian went off to work, I taught, Hunter studied, I did regular household chores. Nothing was exciting about any of that. We went to church. Life continued as expected until November 11, 2020.

CHAPTER 19

Brian, Hunter, and I had gone into the Meijer store to shop. We were getting ready to head to the checkout counters. Suddenly, Brian did not look good. He looked frail and troubled. He looked to be in great pain and struggling. However, he would not be specific. I told him that Hunter and I could finish checking out if he wanted to go to the car.

He did want to and hurriedly left the store. I turned my head to watch him leave. He moved fast but looked frightened. Hunter and I checked out. We went to the car and loaded the groceries into the trunk. Brian said, "I feel like I am having a heart attack. We should go to the ER."

I replied, "I can drive."

Brian refused. "No, I can do it." I was grateful that the hospital was only about half a mile away.

Upon arriving, Brian got out of the car. The security guard quickly got him into the building. Then Hunter and I went to enter the ER waiting room. The hospital was under COVID restrictions and were not allowing children to enter. They asked me to wait in the car, and a nurse would come out and let me know what was going on. I quickly contacted our church. Our friend Stacie agreed to go to the ER parking lot and pick up Hunter. I gave her a key to our home, and she left with Hunter.

Soon, a nurse came to my car and informed me that Brian was having a heart attack. He further explained that they would take him up for a heart cath. They would get me so I could wish him luck before they took him up for the cath. God was so present on this day!

They came to take me into the hospital to see Brian. Upon entering and walking down the hall, I saw that the medical team was rushing Brian to an elevator. I was only able to wave and say, "I love you." Once again, I had to wait. This time, they took me to a room. There were no other people there. This was the room where the doctor would come to explain and show me what and where the problems were in Brian's heart.

The doctor arrived much later. It seemed like an eternity. My whole body felt like I was present in a form of the twilight zone. He showed me where they had found nine blockages in his heart. They were significant. They did not think that they could bypass all the blockages. In addition, three of them were too risky to surgically repair. The other areas were 60 percent to 95 percent blocked. He felt that if the surgery was a success, it would give Brian another fourteen or fifteen years of life. They scheduled his surgery for Friday, November 13, 2020.

Since the hospital did not allow me to see Brian, I returned home. I thanked Stacie and her daughters for taking such great care of Hunter. We discussed the findings before she left to be with her other children. Then I got on the phone with Alexis. I explained that the doctor said I could be at the hospital when Brian had his surgery.

I asked Alexis if Hunter could have a sleepover at their house. Of course, Alexis said yes. This was to be Hunter's first sleepover. It was also Alexis's first time caring for Hunter's hearing aid and cochlear sensory processor system. I took Hunter over to their house Thursday evening. Hunter was so excited. I felt like a zombie explaining how to care for Hunter's hearing apparatuses. I wrote instructions for his medications and the care of his processors. I took foods that I knew he would eat. I felt anxious for Hunter and Brian as I left to go home.

Friday came. I received a call that I could no longer be at the hospital when he had his surgery. Since we were only twenty minutes away, they felt that I could get to the hospital in time if needed. That was simply their way of saying, "In case it looks like he's not going to make it." Hard, hard, hard waiting is an understatement!

I had to deal with notifying our close family members. The hardest one for me was advising Monica. She had ostracized us. She had ignored us and shut us out of her life, and we were sure that she no longer loved us. I struggled with notifying her. Yet I let her know. I created a group text of close family members and included her. She could do whatever she wanted to with that information. I provided all his phone numbers and told them that I would keep them informed and tell them when it would be all right to contact Brian. Now it was up to Monica if she decided to text or call him. Monica never called or texted me. She did contact her dad. Usually, it was merely sharing silly jokes.

The second day, after Brian's bypass surgery, the hospital quarantined Brian. One of his direct care ER team members tested positive for COVID. Now the staff would not allow Brian out of his room. He needed to walk to regain his strength. Brian's quarantine minimized his ability to walk more. On Wednesday, November 18, Brian went code blue twice. The first time, the medical team quickly brought him back. An hour later, he went into the second code blue. They tried CPR on him. CPR did not work. They ended up using the defibrillator. That worked.

Brian and I had talked about downsizing our home for a couple of years. While he was in the hospital, I discussed putting the house on the market with Brian. He agreed with me. I put the house on the market. Alexis's mother happened to be a Realtor. We had recently changed our guardianship choice to Alexis and Nathan, with Belinda as co-guardian.

Alexis's mom, Carrie, met Hunter. Both Carrie and her husband, Gene, quickly fell in love with Hunter. Here again, God stepped in and up! Carrie and Gene had their home on the market. They offered to reduce the price of their home, withdraw it from the market, and sell it to us when our home sold. Brian agreed to my putting the house on the market.

Brian had one medical problem after another during his recovery. His kidneys were failing. The surgery had caused damage to his kidneys. His potassium levels dropped. Finally, Brian did get strong enough to come home. Thanksgiving eve day, Hunter and I went to the hospital to pick him up. We had to wait in the car, at the front entrance, for staff to bring him to us. Then we had to wait again while their pharmacy filled a prescription for him. Finally, we were able to go home.

Brian began the required therapies. He followed most of his restrictions. However, the house was now on the market. We were also going through a 4,400-square-foot home and sorting things. Brian was able to help with small tasks. We had a five-hundred-foot paved driveway. I had never been able to manage the snowblower. It was more like the snowblower controlling me. I know it must have been great fun to watch me, with it winning and me losing the battle. Our lives felt blessed. Our next-door neighbor, Braxton Steele, offered to keep us plowed. To say that the next few months were busy, hectic, and overwhelming is an understatement!

We were sorting. We were donating. We daily made sure the house was clean and orderly. We were going to appointments. Plus, when the Realtor was showing the house, we had to leave. We received an offer on our home after the second showing—just a couple of weeks into the process.

Brian was still restricted. We had a closing date on both our home and the home we were buying, scheduled for March 11, 2021. Carrie and Gene allowed us to move into their home two days before the closing. That allowed Brian and Hunter to set up air mattresses and stay at our soon-to-be new home while I stayed behind and did a deep cleaning.

Our daughter Belinda and her husband, Devan, came and helped load our U-Haul. Earlier, they came with their own U-Haul rental and took our sentimental furnishings. Once again, Braxton Steele helped us. Our cousin's husband, Rob, helped unload our U-Haul trailer. Friends and family helped us through so much. I will forever be grateful.

Mid-April 2021, Hunter was tossing and turning while trying to go to sleep. Soon, I could hear him moaning and thrashing about in his bed. I asked, "Hunter, are you all right?"

He replied, while moaning, "I do not know."

I said, "Why don't you come and lie down with Mama?" He came into bed with me. He continued to moan and toss. Then he began to hyperventilate and placed his hand on the top of his head.

I said to Hunter, "Let's get up. I want to take your blood pressure." We went to the dining room table. I proceeded to take his blood pressure. His blood pressure was 200/128! Hunter was moaning even more, he as whimpering, and he was holding his hand about one inch away from the top of his head. Immediately, I called 911. I requested a medic but asked them to come without sirens.

They had a team of five men when they arrived. First, they thought that our blood pressure cuff might be the problem. The team compared our cuff with theirs. They evaluated ours to be close to their readings. They asked his health history. Upon learning of his history of seizures and having a diagnosis of hypoxic ischemic encephalopathy, they were concerned.

The team stayed and continued to take periodic blood pressure readings with both their equipment and ours. Hunter's blood pressure went down to within the low-high normal range. They considered taking him to the hospital. However, upon learning that we had an appointment with Hunter's neurologist and his primary physician, they decided to not take him to the hospital. One of their main reasons was also because of the high rate of COVID cases at our hospital. However, they decided to run an EKG on Hunter just to be cautious. Upon bringing out the lead wires, Hunter began to grab the wires and tried to help place them onto his chest. He wanted to help them. The team gave a little chuckle. I stated that he was familiar with the process.

The next day, I contacted Hunter's neurologist, Dr. Sam Dodge, and informed him of the previous night's health scare with Hunter. I asked if Hunter may have had a seizure that would have triggered his blood pressure to be high or caused the discomfort in his head. Dr. Dodge stated that it would more likely be due to a heart condition or kidney problem.

Next, Hunter saw Dr. Kelly. Dr. Kelly sent referrals to an endocrinologist, a nephrologist, and a cardiologist. Hunter had lab work, two ultrasounds of his kidneys and adrenal glands, a CAT scan, and an echocardiogram. The lab work showed that his cortisol levels were low. However, the ultrasounds of his kidneys and adrenal glands did not show any irregularities. The endocrinologist then ordered a STIM test. It was to determine if Hunter's body was able to produce his own cortisol or not. The test proved that his body was able to produce cortisol.

The specialists had found nothing with his heart or kidneys that would have caused the problem. Dr. Dodge decided to then order a seventy-two-hour EEG test to be within the Tennessee Children's Hospital. Brian and I had to stay in the room with Hunter. There was a small love seat that turned into a bed within Hunter's room. Brian slept there. I slept in a recliner chair next to Hunter's bed.

The nurses and medical staff hooked up Hunter to the EEG leads, wrapped his head in gauze to hold them in place, and hooked up the monitors to all the equipment. Hunter had brought his little stuffed monkey with him to the hospital. He asked that they wrap his monkey's head. Hunter told the team that the monkey did not want to feel different. The staff kindly wrapped the monkey's head.

During the hospital stay, the children's team entertained the children. They showed educational question-and-answer or bingo on the hospital room's television. The children then used their hospital room phone to call in their answers or claim a bingo. The children then could choose a prize if right or if they won. When it was time to say goodbye and hang up, Hunter would say, "Bye, love you."

One time, a gentleman responded, "We need more of that in this world."

Upon completion of the EEG, the doctor informed us that they did not see any spikes. This only meant that Hunter did not have any seizures. It did not mean that a seizure could not have caused his previous high blood pressure and head-hurting episode. Hunter's primary physician stated that the only diagnosis they could give Hunter, based on that episode, was acute high blood pressure. Thus far, Hunter has had about three episode of acute high blood pressure since then. They have never reached a reading that high, but they have included the pain in the head symptoms.

Early July 2021, Monica called and asked if we were up for a visit. I replied sure. I then asked when and who. She stated that it would be just her. I asked her if she would like to visit "Granny" while she was here. Mom is "Granny" to our children, grandchildren, and friends.

I was sitting on our front deck reading when she arrived. Brian and Hunter were both outdoors. Hunter was curious about roads, so he had his map in his hand. Monica looked like she intended to come up and greet me first. However, Brian and Hunter reached her first. Monica quickly hugged her father, pointed to his chest to ask how his heart was, then gave him a quick hug and told him that she loved him. He did not hear her say that she loved him. I did hear Monica say to him that she did love him.

Hunter then dominated her time with his map. Eventually, they made it up to the front door. We all visited for half an hour. Monica did not have time for an extended visit. We planned to take her to lunch at Applebee's and then see Mom. The conversation was awkward, tense, and limited. Monica teased Hunter and ask him questions about what he liked.

It was nice to see the smile on Mom's face as she visited with Monica. Hunter had fun running around the lawn. Eventually, we said our goodbyes and headed back to our home. Monica had told Hunter that she would like to take him on a road trip someday. Brian and I both knew that we would not allow that soon—if ever.

Hunter asked Monica why she never sent him birthday cards. I do not think she heard him very well because she asked him if he wanted her to sing "Happy Birthday" to him. He said yes. Monica liked to sing the happy birthday song in an extraordinary and purposefully awful tone. She sang it to him. Hunter loved it and told her that. She said, "Thank you. Not many like my birthday song."

It was time for her to leave, and we all gave a quick hug goodbye. A couple of days later, I called Monica. I asked her if she loved me. She replied, "Yes, I do." I told her that I had difficulty believing that she loved me since she had not acknowledged anything I had sent her. Monica had not continued to make any effort to contact us. I then asked her if she knew what message Butch had sent to Tootsie after our visit in 2016. She denied knowing. I do not believe that she did not know. She said nothing that would indicate that she genuinely loved her dad or me. Any communications we receive now are merely initiative taking and superficial.

CHAPTER 20

Pondering. Yes, pondering. I am sitting here, looking at the lakes from the inside of our home. Why am I questioning this journey? I am sure God put us on it. Yet why me? Why us? It does not seem logical. Yet He did.

It is a complex, arduous journey! Am I failing at it? Am I worthy? Am I like Moses, who responded that he did not speak well? I do not know. Yet I press on, albeit not confidently. At least that is my interpretation of what I do or how I react. One day, a good friend at church told me that I was doing a wonderful job. I responded, "Only with God's strength and help. It is God doing the work."

She replied, "Yes, but you did not have to say yes. You could have quit." That was about two years ago.

Lately, I feel like I am reacting in fear, in unjustified anger, and in an unkind manner. We love this little boy who God made clear we were to step up and help, to be an advocate for him. He was our great-grandson. Now, six years later, he is also our son. He will become nine years old this week. He came to us at twenty-seven months of age. He was born hearing impaired. He did not receive the appropriate medical care for his hearing.

Sitting here, I find myself reflecting on and recalling my disgust, anger, and disappointment as I read his medical records.

I have them for his first twenty-seven months of life. Never have I regretted following through and obtaining them. It took several calls reminding our granddaughter to give her authorization to have them sent to us. They are in a three-inch binder now and filed away for safety. I had them all copied and gave the copies to his pediatrician.

Oh, how we wanted our granddaughter to come and live with us. We felt that Deb would receive the counseling that she needed. She might also attend college. She has two other children who live with their biological father and stepmother. The court now allows Deb supervised visits with Annie and Alden. Our offer was there for her to refuse or accept. It remained an open invitation. Unfortunately, she did not choose it.

I am finding my mind wandering and reflecting today. Hunter, who is now our son, later received the following diagnoses: unspecified epileptic, unspecified anxiety, obsessive compulsion disorder, fetal alcohol syndrome, and dyslexia, and he is on the spectrum of autism. Dr. Wollery made all these diagnoses, except the dyslexia, when Hunter was five years of age. We knew that he had failed the hearing test, had no heartbeat upon birth, went into seizures, and was in the NIC unit for eight days. It left him with a history of hypoxic ischemic encephalophagy. I had to look that up! I learned that 60 percent of the children who receive this diagnosis die by age two. The remaining 40 percent end up with other medical conditions. They do not get off free.

Now I am again gazing out of my living room window—still, so many questions and concerns. *Mary, are you convinced that you are all you can and should be for Hunter now? What more should I have done for him and when?* I need to continue to review events again.

Lately, I am finding myself in deep reflection of who I am. A child with a trauma-based past. A child who her mother ostracized. Classmates bullied me as a child because of my last name. My maiden name represented those on my father's side, who were always in trouble to a degree with the law. So much heartache that I did not face squarely. That is, until more so lately. So I ponder. Lord, are You sure that I am the one to help Hunter? Even though this question enters my mind, my heart shouts, "Yes!"

So, with a bit of hesitation and fear, I begin recalling the journey we have been on. My husband and I had been married for fifty years when Hunter became a more significant part of our lives. We were taking care of my aging mother. My mother had lived with us for half of our married life.

In the 1980s, Brian accepted a position in a suburb of Grand Haven, Tennessee. Our three children were in high school. I had a position as a purchasing agent in our area. I was in the middle of a project for Buick City. I resourced the fabricators and material suppliers. Then I shared the available options with the engineers. The engineers were in the process of designing and patenting die manipulators for an automotive manufacturer. Our engineers obtained the patent for both manipulators that we had. The project was not complete. Brian and our three children moved first. I remember how lonely it was coming home to an empty house. However, I followed through and eventually joined them. Brian had purchased a duplex for us to live in. It was only one block from the high school.

When I arrived, we learned more about the area. Eventually, I interviewed and obtained an excellent position with a company in that area. Life was standard. Our children were experiencing behavior problems. They were behaviors experienced by teenagers who came home alone. Today, I advise and inform parents that most teenagers need a parent home when they get out of school for the day. Not only do they need adult supervision, but they also need a parent to listen and be available.

My father and mother had divorced. Dad had obtained a job in the northeastern part of the state. He did remarry. My dad was a heavy smoker, had been exposed to various chemicals, and was an alcoholic. Eventually, those things caught up with his health.

He got cancer. At first, he went to live with my brother. I will not go into the details, but it was not a good environment. Social workers would call on him. The social workers later told me that they had tried to get him to tell them what was going on. Once, he tried to run away from my brothers. Eventually, I offered to have him come and try living with us. We could get doctors for him.

Dad agreed to come. It was so funny. I stocked our cabinets with foods that he liked. I turned a bedroom into a safe and comfortable place for him. We would take him to doctors, to church, and to visit car dealers. He always liked to look at cars. I am shaking my head in amusement. One day, I took Dad to a car dealership. I stood behind Dad so he could not see what I was saying. I was prepared to explain that Dad could not buy a car. The salespeople were always good sports.

Dad had only been with us for three days when he said, "Let's go!"

"Go where?" I replied.

He responded, "Up north and to the attorneys. I want to stay with you."

"OK, Dad. Are you sure?" I replied. He said that he was. So off we went. The lawyer completed and filed the necessary legal documents. Dad continued to become weaker after we returned to our home. Oh, the trips we made to the ER! Dad was happy with us and determined to be there. Mom came one time and visited him. He had never really stopped loving her. He often shared that he had regretted much. Dad lived only about three months longer. That is too long of a story to share. Suffice it to say that I had my hands full with legal things to take care of after his death.

Shortly after that, Mom's health began to fail. She had been working as a quality manager at a factory. She ended up having to quit. Again, we had her come visit, and we took her to doctors. The doctors diagnosed Mom with diabetes and heart issues. She was behind in her property taxes, and her furnace had failed. Brian and I paid for her furnace to be replaced.

When our children graduated, we decided to move back up north. Brian had a job that was demanding and often required thirty hours of overtime. He was in quality engineering at a middle management level. His manager simply procrastinated when providing information about the next deadline. He sent out his résumé, received an interview, and the rest is history. Off we went up north.

We asked Mom if we could buy her house and give her a lifetime lease to live there and move in. She agreed. These were events that led to Mother living with us for half of our married life.

CHAPTER 21

Still reflecting, I pause again to explain why I am questioning this journey. Hunter is eight years old and has been asking questions lately. The questions have been about Brian's and my childhood. He would ask, "Where you lived, what kind of bedroom did you have? Was your mama and papa kind?" and more.

This past summer, he asked me his mother's and father's names. I decided to tell Hunter all truths in an age-appropriate manner and at the right time(s). The question about his parents' names led to this conversation: I said, "Hunter, I am not going to give you their names right now. I will tell you when you are about twelve years old."

Hunter asked, "Is my mom a good mom?"

I replied, "Hunter, she loved you very much. She did not know how to be a good parent. Remember when Ms. Alexis and Mr. Nathan decided to adopt? Well, often parents love their children. Yet they do not know how to be a good parent. So other people, like Ms. Alexis and Mr. Nathan, will say, 'That is OK. We will step up and love and protect them.'"

Hunter replied, "Yes, that is nice of them. What about my dad? Is he a good guy?"

I said, "No, he is bad. He hurt children. He has been in jail for a long time. It is a prison."

Hunter asked, "How did he hurt children?"

I replied, "Hunter, someday I will tell you. Today is not the time to talk about it. I will tell you everything when it is the right time."

That was a difficult conversation. Yet it was not the trigger for my questioning things. The motivation came one day about two months ago. We were riding in the car. Hunter once again was asking us about things from our childhood. We were answering him honestly. That is, until I could not answer. Hunter had asked me what kind of bedroom I had growing up.

I did not expect Hunter's question to create an emotional trigger. I froze and simply said that I could not answer that right now. I could not tell him that I usually had a bedroom of my own. Now, that sounds like it should be a wonderful thing, especially since I was one of six siblings. I am the oldest of six children. My mother would find a way to give me my room. It was not often that Mom would allow me to play with my siblings. For the first time, I realized that my mom had ostracized me from our family. I knew she had. I am just beginning to understand or recognize it more—yet not completely.

I could not talk with Hunter anymore about my childhood for the rest of that day. I made a lame excuse that I had to think about where we were going or for what I had to shop. It does not matter. He was content to question Brian.

I sat, riding in silence, while my mind and my heart were sorting out my emotions. Suddenly, I did not feel worthy. I did not feel valued. I did not believe that anyone could love me, not even this little boy who constantly said, "I love you, Mama. I love you so, so much! Do you love me?" I always answer, "Yes, I do!"

I began examining and questioning my emotions. I found myself thinking about how I had managed past experiences. One of the first experiences that entered my memory was taking our children to a blind Christian psychologist. We were noticing behavioral problems. He spoke with Brian and me first. Then he met with our children individually.

When it was my turn to enter his office alone, he asked me about my childhood. He asked me about my siblings. He asked me about my parents. I was truthful. My dad loved his children, but he was an alcoholic. He worked on ships that were lower lakers. He was often away for weeks working. Often, he would get his paycheck and spend it on alcohol and women. Sometimes he came home with a bit of money, and we could buy groceries. I shared how, at age eight, I took my dad for a walk. I shared that I told Dad that he needed to bring home money to purchase food. I continued to share that I had to be a grown-up at the age of eight. I had to be grown-up in more ways than I would have wished. I never doubted that my dad loved me. Mom, well, she expected me to take care of the other children. If I did not do so, she would kick me to the ground, hit me, or do something else. Once, she chased me with a two-by-four!

These are things that I shared. I then shared things about my sister Lydia. I also shared what led to my sister Lydia committing suicide. I learned of her suicide on our ninth wedding anniversary. It was then that I also learned that one of Lydia's counselors had stated if a counselor had diagnosed my father, he would have been diagnosed as schizophrenic. When I finished sharing these things and more, the psychologist said, "Mary, you are not a robot. You need to learn to be still and let God. You will always not trust that others love you. Be still and let God."

Oh my, how I reacted to that remark! It made me angry! I will never forget my reaction. I can still see my response. I still feel it! I responded by stomping my feet rapidly up and down. This is what I was yelling through tears. "I cannot do that. I cannot *be still!*" My reaction stunned me! I could not believe that I reacted in that manner. I was both embarrassed and ashamed.

Presently, I am more still. Yet there are days when the triggers happen. Remarkably, there are days when I can recall who did love me well during my childhood. My elderly cousin, who we lovingly called Uncle Doc, was a pastor. I could share things with him. I could ask him questions. He always had a simple answer.

While I was in the eighth grade, one exchange we had stuck with me. I treasure it. I had been hearing my name called every night when in bed. I shared that I was hearing someone call my name. Only my name. Uncle Doc replied, "Just say, 'Lord, here I am.'" I did that the next night. I felt a sense of peace, and I never heard my name like that again. Not until much later while growing up and taking college classes. I may share that experience later.

I am beginning to realize that God may be using Hunter to also heal and lead me closer to God. Just beginning.

CHAPTER 22

Mary is again thinking and remembering. Hunter was scheduled for his Tennessee U of M visit on September 16, 2021. It was for testing and reprogramming his cochlear sensory processor with the audiologist team. After the audiologist team finished, his speech pathologist was to evaluate Hunter's development. The speech pathologist's testing lasted from one to two hours.

The pathologist used four to six books containing different pictures. The books usually had images that allowed the tester to make a statement and follow it with a question. With two books, the speech pathologist was allowed to repeat the sequence statement and question or rephrase the comment and question. The other three to four books did not qualify for a repeat or rephrase.

On this visit, a new speech pathologist evaluated Hunter. Hunter was not familiar with her. This led to a change in routine for Hunter. He began to be in one of his silly imaginary play modes. In addition, he was not able to focus on the presentations appropriately. His noncompliance and ridiculous responses continued to escalate. He was deliberately making errors.

One of his goals is to buy a blue pickup truck when he becomes sixteen. The next picture that the pathologist showed Hunter was a picture of a red pickup truck. She asked what he saw. His response was, "A blue pickup truck," which he then followed by elaborating on his blue pickup truck. His hands were in autistic motion and excitement. However, it was also undeniable that his behaviors resulted from deliberate noncompliance. I will say that he was indeed tired as well, which surely did not help the situation.

So I was sitting there observing all his behaviors. My heart was devastated! We had poured so much into Hunter! I had poured so much into Hunter. He had come so far! His previous assessment had shown an eighteen-month gain within six months. Tears were streaming down my face. I was fighting sobs. Gently, I periodically wiped away the tears. Occasionally, I turned my head so Hunter could not see my reactions. Gently, I rocked in the chair. I wanted to run out. I wanted to help Hunter or coax him. Yet it was not appropriate. It felt like forever. I knew I must be failing Hunter! I knew it. I felt so broken! The pathologist was finishing with the testing. She informed us that Hunter had lost ground and was now back into the severely delayed category. Seriously?

We left and made an appointment for six months later. Up to this point, Hunter's appointment schedule had been once a year. However, this appointment went so poorly that the medical team felt he needed to return in six months.

We walked out to our car. Hunter and Brian got into the car. I collapsed onto the hood of our car and began to sob. I could not stop crying! "I am done! I cannot do this!" I said while sobbing. I tried pulling myself together and getting into the car. I knew that my reaction was not good for Hunter. I had to get it together. Yet I felt so broken. So unworthy. Such a failure.

I got into the car. Hunter said in a gentle and calm voice, "Mama, you do not need to cry. Stop crying. Calm your body down." My words came right back at me. I was still crying, but he did not hear or see me. I was proud of his calm demeanor. Yet I was broken! I knew, at that moment, that I had failed Hunter somehow.

Riding home, I wanted to die. I wanted to end it all. I thought, *If I simply open the door and jump out while on the freeway, I will be killed. I could do that. It would be quick.* Then I reasoned with myself, *But God. But Hunter. That would be so traumatic for him. It is not what God would agree to.* I opened my FB to a particular journey group and posted. "I am so broken!" That was all.

Immediately, I received a phone call from a dear friend. She asked me what was up. I simply would not and could not share with her. We were all in the car driving. Hunter should not hear what I would share. The tears began again. Hunter heard my crying, and I simply kept replying, "Alexis, I cannot talk about it right now." Of course, later, I shared all the events that led up to my reactions and the details of those reactions.

After the call ended, Hunter, once again calming, said, "Mama, calm your body down. You do not need to cry."

After we returned home, I decided to take a walk by myself. Then another dear and trustworthy friend, Donna Fry, called. Donna reminded and encouraged me, "Mary, you know that's just Satan talking." I did agree with her but still felt so broken. Even though feeling so broken, I knew that I would never, *never ever* commit suicide. I knew that God had put us on this journey. Donna ended our conversation praying over me and us. Such a sweet and strong lady who understands how difficult it is to raise grandchildren.

That was the day I began the process of questioning my part in Hunter's journey. I was evaluating the value of my existence. I can confidently say God is teaching me to trust Him more. It was becoming more apparent that I was not acknowledging God was already controlling our paths. I am sure that He has slapped me right back onto His potter's wheel.

CHAPTER 23

I purchased all of Hunter's third-grade curriculum. I intended to continue homeschooling him. One homeschooling day, Hunter began to make errors deliberately. I knew it to be deliberate because he was making mathematical errors—mistakes that a kindergartener would not have made.

Hunter was going into his creative and imaginative mode. That is one of his autistic characteristics. However, he chose to refocus and did continue to make deliberate errors. I decided it was time to place him back into the public school system. At first, I said to Hunter, "Obviously, you need a new teacher. I am done teaching you today. School is now finished. So, you need to teach yourself today." Hunter looked at me, puzzled. I proceeded to put out the large dry erase whiteboard and markers.

"Hunter," I began, "you are going to work on your alphabet all over again. Please write both as both upper and lowercase letters. Tell me when you have finished." I then left the room. Hunter was excited! One of his chosen professions is to become a teacher. I could hear him speaking the letters aloud to himself. Suddenly, he began to pretend to instruct other children. Silently, I chucked. I was still trying to stifle my anger at his previous deliberate errors.

I allowed Hunter to continue this way for about an hour. Afterward, I permitted him to have a recess break. After I gave

Hunter his allowed free time, I cleaned the whiteboard. "Hunter," I said, "I will put math problems on the whiteboard. You are to solve them yourself. Please remember to proof your work." Once again, I left the room.

I no longer wondered if Hunter needed to be back in the public school system. I knew that he needed additional points of view presented to him. Hunter also needed different socialization. I made an appointment to meet the Blue Mountain Elementary school principal. Hunter and I went to the meeting. We arrived prepared with records, letters from his medical team, and a written request to schedule a new IEP meeting.

I provided additional reasons we pulled Hunter from his first-grade class. I informed him we had not shared those reasons with the previous school and their staff. Mr. Gray needed to understand that I would always choose to win the war. Going to battle would not win the war for Hunter. Upon receiving additional information, Mr. Gray agreed to allow Hunter to attend. The required meetings and team were prepared for Hunter to participate on September 27, 2021.

Hunter acclimated exceptionally well. His team stated, "Kudos to you, mom, and dad. Hunter has adjusted better than other students who attended virtually during COVID." He still struggles academically. Yet his focus and attention have improved. The state-required timed testing puts Hunter in the third percentile. We also have Hunter enrolled in Sylvan.

I was so concerned about the third percentile evaluation. I decided to contact Sylvan. I met with Lisa and discussed my concerns. She replied, "Mary, these tests are not comparing apples to apples. Hunter is autistic. We know that he is capable. However, the tests are testing oranges to apples. You also need to realize Hunter is always going to be different."

Yes, it is a truth that I need to accept. I believe that I always have accepted that fact. However, I will never give up helping him become the best he can become. If he becomes the kindest, most compassionate person and capable of higher achievement, that will be enough. I know that his character is noble. He has noble goals. Hunter will work to become a great husband, father, and either an employee or an employer.

Hunter's goals do change. His heart, so far, has been so kindly focused. Some of his goals are to own a blue pickup, a trailer to pull a boat, and a motor home; to teach preschool, kindergarten, and first grade; to build and own a factory; to live on a two-track road in Blue Lake Mountain; to marry Carrie Lyn and have two biological children, to have a girl first and to name her Annie, and to adopt ten children. He wants to adopt so that he and his wife can step up and protect children whose parents do not know how to parent.

Within those goals are more well-defined attributes and reasons: the pickup must have a cross because he believes in Jesus; the factory must be named Seiki; his factory is to make new items that look like old technology but perform in a modern technological manner; it must have a mall attached; the mall is to include a Christian school, a daycare, a doctor's office, and a grocery store (the facilities within the mall are for the convenience of his future employees); and his factory is to be in Blue Mountain.

CHAPTER 24

This time, my pondering leads me to a place of contentment. God loves His children, and I am one of His. He has promised me that He will finish the work He began in us.

Indeed, my childhood experiences left me sometimes lonely, ostracized at times, abused, insecure, and with few real friendships. I regret that those experiences and others did not allow me to parent as well as I should have with our first three children. My parenting style was characterized by fear—fear that they might become like my father's side of the family. I now understand that I should be grateful that they survived my worries as I parented them. God was merciful. He is yet merciful.

Brian knew that recognizing my mother had ostracized me was causing me sorrow. This past week, we visited my mother at the Brookside. Unexpectedly to me, Brian asked my mother, "Do you remember why you always gave Mary a room of her own?"

Mom replied, "I do not know. She always was able to keep things neat. I never even had to teach her to get ready for school in kindergarten. She just stepped up on the stool and got herself ready. She always kept her room neat and in order. She was just *fussy!*"

Brian replied, "Oh."

Mom continued, "If I would have put her in the room with the other kids … well, that would not have worked out! She was just too fussy!" Then she merely sighed. Brian was trying to find a way to help me not feel ostracized. I appreciated his concern.

However, I also have a letter she wrote to my siblings years ago. She had found it when she was packing to go into assisted living. She brought it for me to see and read. I began to read it when she left. It made me sad. Yet I asked her if I could have the letter to keep. She said that I could. In that letter, Mom explained to my siblings that "Mary is not so bad. She wants to have family over for holidays and dinners. She is not so bad." My siblings had not wanted Mom to sell us her home.

I have been reminding myself of Proverbs 3:5–6: "Trust in the Lord with all your heart and do not lean unto your understanding. In all your ways, acknowledge me, and I will direct your path."

Remember, Mary, when you take the time to look back, you will see the times that He came through powerfully. I remember the abscessed tooth Monica had when she was young. It cost a lot of money to repair. Brian was unemployed. We were getting ready to go to church Wednesday evening. *Monica approached you. She said that her tooth hurt. Mary, you looked inside and recognized another abscess. You then had Brian look at it for confirmation. He recognized it too.*

You walked up and down the hallway, getting things ready to leave for church. You began to talk aloud to God. You were saying, "God, why is this happening? You know that we cannot afford this! Why now!" About five minutes later, you asked to look into Monica's mouth. The abscess was completely gone! The lesson you learned that day: God is listening! Even when you do not talk to Him respectfully.

Also, remember, Mary: driving to your college Economics 101 class. What did you say while you were driving? You do remember! You started yelling while you were driving. "God why am I taking this class! What good is it ever going to do for me?

How will I be using it in my life? This is crazy! I have a test tonight. It is hard! I am in my thirties, attending with a group of students who came in saying that they chose this class last because it is hard. Why am I doing this?"

Then a male's voice replied, "Mary, when it is time, you will be able to use this."

You recall questioning, "Was that just God talking to me?" Years later, you did use economics often.

Do not forget, even though your mother chased you with the two-by-four, she did not catch you. You did not get beaten that day. God saw you. He protected.

Remember, the bullies may have hurt your heart, but they did not kill your confidence to succeed. Nor did they remove you from your belief in God.

Yes, I do remember! My belief continues to grow. God continues to put me on His potter's wheel. It is good to grow. God's potter's wheel creates good change.

CHAPTER 25

Indeed, here I am in my reflective moments yet again. Yes, there are and will be times when I consider myself unworthy. I am one of God's children. Yes, I am. Am I occasionally a disobedient child? Oh my, yes!

I am a little like Moses at times. I can unconditionally state that I was a little like King David and even Abraham or Thomas. Yet our merciful God knows my heart. He chose Brian and me to step up for our great-grandson, Hunter. We did not realize the things that we had yet to learn.

No, it was not a joyful experience watching Hunter suffer through necessary tests. I had to dig deep into my soul to find the strength to patiently model and teach Hunter that families can love, be kind, know and understand God's love, and learn from one another.

I learned to advocate at both the local and state level. There is much more work needed. Laws need changes to protect these children and the senior citizens who step up and into these children's lives. If only governmental units understood that resources are necessary to help with mental health issues and special medical needs.

If a senior citizen adopts outside of the foster care system, their income and assets eventually may do one or two things; if not both: cause the child to lose paid governmental health insurance or the senior citizen to lose the ability to retain what finances they have or hoped to have in their retirement years. The ability to earn income, which would assist in helping them to enjoy their aged years, put away for their adopted son's future, and still be contributing by paying federal and state taxes. Government has much to learn. They often complicate laws by adding unrelated items or ignoring potential pitfalls.

It is time to do a quick recap of where Hunter's development has grown from. He came at twenty-seven months of age, happy, hearing little in his right ear, profoundly deaf in his left ear, displaying OCD and autistic characteristics, with anxieties, timid and mostly nonverbal.

At twenty-eight months of age, he had tubes put into his ears, had a sedated ABR (automated brain response test), and had his first appointment with an audiologist.

At thirty-two months of age, he received his right hearing aid, was in regular speech therapy, and had an Early On intervention team helping him, Brian, and me.

After age three, he continued in speech therapy, began occupational therapy, started seeing a neurologist at the Tennessee Children's Hospital, received his first EEG, and started the process to receive a cochlear implant in his left ear.

At age four, he was in the Great Start Readiness Program, received EEGs, CAT scans, and MRIs, and had the surgery for his cochlear implant. The Tennessee U of M provided Hunter's cochlear implant preparation appointments, follow-up appointments, and cochlear implant surgery.

His most significant event (only in my heart) was us adopting him. Hunter has challenges that will continue with him as he continues to mature. With God's help, I will learn additional ways to help him conquer them. My beginning goal was for Hunter's life to glorify God. I continue to trust that God will lead me and lead to me those who can help us get him to my initial goal for Hunter.

If you were to meet Hunter today, you would be listening to his questions: What brand of TV do you have? Is it LG or Samsung? Do you have Netflix or Hulu? Do you pay for it? Depending on your answer, you could expect to be listening to Hunter for an extended period.

I will never forget Hunter having the following conversation with me: "Mama, do you think you will die today?"

I replied, "Hunter, I do not think so. Maybe. Only God knows when we are going to die. People who love God get to go up and live with Him there."

I was not sure what would come out of Hunter's mouth next or how I might have to manage my response. This is what he said next: "Mama, I think that when you die, the angels will come down and carry you up to heaven." I recall feeling a little choked up and proud of his heart.

Mary, you and Brian provide so much security. You always greet Hunter with a good morning routine. Sometimes it is merely a great big hug. Other times, it is a hug followed by you rubbing your noses together and saying, "Hugga Mugga."

So, am I worthy? God chose us. I believe that God will not only provide direction but also grow us up in Him. We have yet to see where God will lead us next.

EPILOGUE

So, I ponder, "Lord, are You sure that I am the one to help Hunter?"
Even though this question enters my mind, my heart shouts, "Yes!"

Printed in the United States
by Baker & Taylor Publisher Services